Better Homes and Gardens®

Low-Maintenance
Gardening Made Easy

Meredith Consumer Marketing
Des Moines, Iowa

Better Homes and Gardens Low-Maintenance Gardening Made Easy

MEREDITH CONSUMER MARKETING
Consumer Marketing Product Director: Heather Sorensen
Consumer Marketing Product Manager: Wendy Merical
Consumer Marketing Billing/Renewal Manager: Tami Beachem
Business Director: Ron Clingman
Senior Production Manager: Al Rodruck

WATERBURY PUBLICATIONS, INC.
Contributing Editor: Karen Weir-Jimerson, Studio G, Inc.
Contributing Copy Editor: Peg Smith
Contributing Proofreader: Gretchen Kauffman
Contributing Indexer: Donald Glassman
Editorial Director: Lisa Kingsley
Creative Director: Ken Carlson
Associate Editors: Tricia Bergman, Mary Williams, Annie Peterson
Associate Design Director: Doug Samuelson
Production Assistant: Mindy Samuelson

BETTER HOMES AND GARDENS MAGAZINE
Editor in Chief: Stephen Orr
Managing Editor: Gregory H. Kayko
Creative Director: Jennifer D. Madara
Deputy Editor, Garden: Jane Austin Miller

MEREDITH NATIONAL MEDIA GROUP
President: Tom Harty

MEREDITH CORPORATION
Chairman and Chief Executive Officer: Stephen M. Lacy

In Memoriam: E.T. Meredith III (1933–2003)

Pictured on the front cover:
top left Easy-care roses are a beautiful addition to gardens and landscapes.
bottom left Grow modern and heirloom vegetables in your backyard with low-maintenance methods.
right Perennials offer foliage and flower in every season, plus they come back year after year.

Copyright © 2016
Meredith Corporation.
Des Moines, Iowa.
First Edition.
Printed in the United States of America.
ISBN: 978-0696-30235-0

All of us at Meredith Consumer Marketing are dedicated to providing you with information and ideas to enhance your home. We welcome your comments and suggestions. Write to us at: Meredith Consumer Marketing, 1716 Locust St., Des Moines, IA 50309-3023.

Contents

Chapter 1

Chapter 2

Chapter 3

Chapter 4

Chapter 5

70 MINIMIZING GARDEN WORK

A low-maintenance plan makes gardening less time-consuming.

Chapter 6

132 THE EASIEST PLANTS

Start with easy-care plants and you'll have a beautiful garden without the fuss.

Chapter 7

180 LOW-MAINTENANCE CONTAINERS

Create beautiful easy-care gardens in pots for patios and decks.

Chapter 8

196 EASY-CARE GARDEN PLANS

Start with an easy-care garden plan and your garden will nearly care for itself.

CHAPTER ONE

The Keys to Low Maintenance

An easy-care garden can be yours
with some simple planning.

Benefits of Low-Maintenance Gardening

The amount of time spent in your garden should be determined by you, not your plants.

Gardening is a hobby that gives back in unexpected ways. That's why it is one of the most popular outdoor activities; however, not everyone wants to spend a ton of time working in the garden in order to enjoy it. For the time-squeezed among us, there are many ways to shave off work time in the garden. This book will show you how to plan and garden successfully without spending more time than you want. You may find as your experience with gardening grows that you'll add to your landscape, beds, and borders and that the amount of time you spend planting, harvesting, and admiring will also grow each year.

What kind of garden do you want?

Gardens are many things to many people. They can be beautiful flower borders, fragrant and colorful sideyard niches, spiritually nurturing herb beds, and plots of ground that yield nutritious organic fruits and vegetables. Deciding what type of garden you want will help make it low-maintenance. For example, if you want to grow herbs, planting them in a container with a drip irrigation system means you won't have to till the ground, build a raised bed, and weed and water every day. Thinking about what you want from your garden will help develop a plan to make it easy to care for and a joy to spend time in.

So how do you do this? It starts with creating expectations. You don't take up a sport such as running or swimming and expect to run a marathon or swim in a triathlon a week after you take up one of them. If you look at gardening as a hobby, and a lifelong hobby at that, expect that there will be things to learn and discover over time. And you'll find the more successes you have, the more time you will want to spend in the garden.

Balancing benefit and time

The benefits of gardening are well documented. Growing plants makes you feel relaxed, connects you to the earth, gives you satisfaction, encourages time outdoors, and burns calories. But many people don't have time to dive into the hobby of gardening like it's a full-time job. For those gardeners, there's hope. You can easily have a beautiful garden and an enviable landscape when you take steps in planning, planting, and maintenance that will reduce the time you work in your garden and increase the time you enjoy and dream in your garden.

What is low-maintenance?

Low-maintenance is a relative term. For some, watering a windowbox once a day is the right amount of gardening commitment. For others, spending time weeding, harvesting vegetables and herbs, and picking bouquets for an hour a day is time well spent. In figuring what you want in a low-maintenance garden, also think about the ratio of time you want to spend and the outcome you want.

Also determine what gardening actually means to you. Thinking about the type of garden that you want will help create one that will meet expectations without overextending on time. Will you be happy with a minimalist landscape of shrubs? Do you want to grow your own vegetables? How do you feel about mowing and weeding? Answering these questions will help determine how to start a low-maintenance garden. Determining what kind of garden and landscape you want, and how much time you'd like to spend in it, will determine how to approach creating the garden of your dreams.

opposite, left Using easy-care groundcover plants instead of labor-intensive lawn makes for a low-maintenance front yard. **opposite, above** Planting drought-tolerant perennials, such as sedum and ornamental grass, requires less watering. **opposite, middle** Low-growing 'Orange Sprite' sanvitalia is an easy-care annual that flowers all summer. **opposite, below** Growing a mass of drought-tolerant succulents in a bowl is as trendy as it is easy.

Style and Planning

The best and most interesting gardens have a strong sense of place that reflects where you live. Rough out a plan to determine the number of plants you will need.

Garden design trends come and go, but gardens that honor regional climates transform with the seasons. Adapting styles to suit the realities of climate and site is vital to garden health and appearance. This is easier if we choose native plants that have already adapted and experiment with others that need help adjusting. For instance, incorporating local stone in your garden ties it into the surroundings naturally.

Your ideal garden

Create your garden according to a specific style or focus on qualities that reflect the character of your home, personality, or lifestyle. Ideally, a sense of style unifies house and garden, providing an outlet for personal expression. What do you see in the garden of your dreams? Does it match the view outside your windows? When you make a garden as a place for you, your family, and friends, it can serve whatever purpose you desire. Private refuge, relaxing room, play place, food source, or wildlife haven—it's your call.

As you make or remake your garden, consider how your garden can work for you. Let it solve a problem where a living fence replaces continual painting chores or where easy-care grasses disguise an unsightly air-conditioner. Look for ways to add comfort, convenience, energy efficiency, property value, privacy, and living space—plants and gardens can do all that and more. Above all, gardens are places of transcendent beauty that give meaning to lives.

Cottage Style
A penchant for plants shows in dense plantings: Favorite flowers and shrubs mix informally with practical edibles and structures.

Easy-Care Style
Taking a simplified approach yields a garden where less is more: Waterwise perennials team with shrubs and trees.

Casual Style
A sleek and eco-chic design works with nature, using native plants that need no pampering and little water.

Formal Style
An urban lifestyle calls for bold architectural plants that provide artful elements by way of containers in limited space.

Making plans for your garden

Putting a garden plan on paper makes sense. It puts you in the position of looking at your yard from a bird's-eye view. Instead of getting bogged down with details, you can play with possibilities.

A simple sketch and a few measurements on paper will do. Whether you're planning a container garden, a bed, or an entire yard, a plan provides a useful reference. Take it with you to the nursery when you select new plants. Let it tell you how much mulch you'll need to order. Your garden plan will help you log progress and decide about changes as your garden grows and evolves.

Before you dig

Plan before planting. Rough out a planting scheme and use it to determine the size and quantity of plants you will need. Then refer to the plan when adding plants to the garden and use it as a future reference.

Take inventory and consider your garden's existing features. What works and doesn't work in the current scheme? Has a tree matured and turned a once full-sun area into a place that needs more plants for dry shade?

Best-laid plans

You might save time and money in the long run by hiring a landscape designer to develop a garden plan. Many nurseries offer free service with purchase of plants. A good designer translates your wishes into a plan that you can bring to life.

LOW-MAINTENANCE GARDENING TIP

PLAN YOUR EASY-CARE KITCHEN GARDEN

Think about how you plan to use your kitchen garden. Besides raising fresh produce within steps of the kitchen door, do you also want to include a place to serve meals, grill, or store tools? Before you plant, gather ideas for structures and planting to help you make the best use of the space.

CALL BEFORE YOU DIG

Call 811 before you dig and request free service to mark underground utility locations. Prevent costly damage to natural gas, cable service, or phone lines with a quick call.

left Choose budget materials. Concrete blocks, gravel, pressure-treated wood, inexpensive pavers, and terra-cotta pots are among materials that fit tight budgets.
above At the top of your gardening to-do list, keep these words: Enjoy the garden. The hottest days of summer are among the best times to put up your feet and just relax. Set aside tools and savor what you have accomplished. Take time to figure out a game plan for fall.

Time and Money

Create and maintain a beautiful garden and still have plenty of time to enjoy it. Gardeners have a reputation as a thrifty and resourceful lot—and we enjoy living up to it.

LOW-MAINTENANCE GARDENING TIP

DISCOVER INSPIRATION FOR YOUR GARDEN

If you have not gardened before, look for design and planting ideas in public gardens, garden center displays, magazines, books, and blogs. Take local garden tours. Focus on a theme, a collection, a vacation spot, or works of a favorite garden writer as a jumping-off point for your garden design.

Gardening smarter instead of harder enables you to have the garden you want without straining yourself to achieve it. In this busy, busy world, gardening offers a respite and an opportunity for relaxing—even in the midst of weeding or mowing.

Swap part of any hectic day for a little quality time in the garden. Not enough time often means too much hassle or effort. Instead of focusing on time constraints, look for ways to make that chore easier, more efficient, and less demanding. Choose gardening as daily or weekly me time, as essential to well-being as exercise. Garden for exercise and double your pleasure. The goal is not to have a perfect garden, but an enjoyable one.

Time-saving strategies

No garden is carefree, but a low-maintenance garden can be yours. Time- and money-saving tips appear throughout this book to help reduce work and expense and enjoy your garden more. Get started with these tips:

Focus on developing one or two key garden areas that offer impact rather than multiple beds and borders in all corners of your property.

Group plants according to their needs. Clustering containers simplifies watering, plus it allows pots to shade each other, which reduces watering. Grouping acid-loving plants means you can acidify the soil more efficiently.

Choose easy-care plants, including shrubs, groundcovers, and perennials that grow well in your area and practically take care of themselves. These are the plants that bring color and character to the garden throughout the growing season and maybe even year-round.

Do little and often, making gardening part of your routine and keeping up with what needs doing. Water houseplants every Friday morning, for instance. Regularly doing part of bigger jobs—weeding, pruning, mulching—minimizes them.

Stretch your dollars

Gardening presents countless ways to spend money on new plants, gleaming tools, must-have do-dads, and other supplies. Of course, you can spend lots of money on a garden, but most of us do the opposite. Frugality is a watch word among gardeners.

We always look for ways to stretch dollars—planting seeds to grow food or waiting until the end of the season to snap up deals on leftover fertilizer and broken bags of soil. Gardeners could show how to repurpose milk jugs into umpteen garden helpers, from plant tags to season-extending cloches. Here are some thrifty gardening tips:

Invest in your soil. Improve and build soil with compost and other amendments. Ensure the money for plants is well spent by putting time, energy, and dollars into making healthy soil. It will show in your garden's success.

Propagate plants. Start plants from seeds and cuttings. Divide and replant perennials you already have before buying more.

Go green to save green. Recycle kitchen and yard waste into gardeners' gold—compost—free soil enrichment. A rain barrel, rain garden, and irrigation conserve water and shrink your water bill.

Divide and conquer. Share skills, time, tools, space, and other resources with gardeners in your community. Share the fun and bounty.

Reduce energy bills. Plant shade trees. Invest in a single tree rather than spending the same amount of money on annuals and perennials. Trees also increase property value.

Sunlight matters. How much sun or shade does the site receive? How much light does the plant need?

Size How big will the plant be at maturity? How much space is needed between it and adjacent plants for growth and adequate air circulation?

Soil Does the soil contain the air, nutrients, and water needed by plants to grow and thrive? Can the plant tolerate a wet or dry site?

Hardiness Is the plant rated for your hardiness zone? Check the plant tag for hardiness information.

Heat and Humidity Can the plant withstand these added challenges? Will it continue to bloom or fruit?

Plants and Light

However much you love a plant, it won't thrive in unsuitable conditions.

Matching plants to the growing conditions of your site is key to creating a beautiful garden with low-maintenance plants. If your garden poses problematic areas—dense shade, slope, boggy spots, hot and dry places—find plants that can cope with the challenge. In the long run, unsuitable plants only mean more work for you.

Consider these practical factors when you choose plant varieties and make sure they are appropriate: size, soil, hardiness, heat, and humidity. Once you assess your site's sun and shade patterns, match plants to those places.

Full-sun equals at least six hours of direct sun daily.

Part-sun/part-shade equals at least three to six hours of sun daily and sites that receive filtered or dappled light.

Full shade equals less than three hours of sun daily.

UNDERSTAND PLANT GROUPS

Different types of plants provide gardeners with essential materials. It helps to understand the terms of what you buy and tend. Make informed choices of plants when you're aware of what each one adds to a garden and how it behaves.

1. PERENNIAL Garden mainstays, the huge array of plants (including Japanese iris) fills beds with shape, color, texture, and fragrance. They often die to the ground during winter but live on for years.

2. BULB Hardy bulbs stay in the ground year-round. Tender bulbs must be dug in freezing climates. Plant spring-flowering bulbs in fall; summer-flowering bulbs in fall or spring.

3. ANNUAL An annual completes its life cycle in a year. The plant begins from a seed, then focuses its energy into flowering and setting seeds.

4. SHRUB As an essential part of a garden, shrubs work as accents and hedges. Deciduous or evergreen shrubs offer seasonal appeal and long-term interest.

5. TREE Evergreen (those that keep foliage) or deciduous (those that drop foliage) trees bring height, shape, and a long-lived framework to the landscape. Trees add shade, shelter, and large-scale seasonal beauty.

6. TURFGRASS North American lawns include cool- and warm-climate plants that need repeated cutting. Practical and pretty lawns include a blend of suitable grass types.

7. CLIMBER OR VINE Annual or perennial, these versatile plants climb, sprawl, and cling. Whether fast- or slow-growing plants, they add verticality to the garden.

Picking Healthy Plants

Take time to read labels and research plants before you buy instead of choosing the most eye-catching plants. Be a smart shopper: Get the healthiest plants at reasonable prices

When to shop

Sales are highest during spring—peak planting season. By the end of June, seasonal garden centers close. Shop early for best choices, but be prepared for full prices and crowds. Garden centers stock up on weekdays. Get the best selection and quality by shopping before the weekend rush, when only picked-over goods remain. If you prefer to hold out for bargains, wait until late June or late summer, when nurseries slash prices.

Where to shop

Local garden centers range from seasonal outlets that buy plants from wholesalers to nurseries and greenhouses that grow their own selections. Specialized nurseries offer plants that you might not find elsewhere.

Catalogs and websites expand plant choices, especially for unusual plants and seeds, roses, trees, and shrubs. Settle on a few good sources to save on shipping costs. Avoid getting caught up in the allure of catalog or online descriptions. Make your wish list, set it aside for a few days, then edit before placing your order.

Reputable garden centers dedicated to long-term care of plants guarantee purchases. If the plant fails within a year, they replace it or refund your purchase (depending on policy) with proof of purchase. Save plant tags with receipts.

What to buy

You'll find generic versions of plants and patent-protected varieties. Patented varieties may cost a little more, but they're a good buy if you get better winter hardiness, disease resistance, or a space-saving form. Generic plants may vary in appearance, while named varieties have consistent characteristics.

Choosing healthy plants

Keep low-maintenance in mind when choosing plants. Healthy plants ensure a more care-free garden. Follow these tips:

Opt for plants with buds over those with flowers.

Check roots by gently removing the pot. Extremely dense, tangled, or dark roots are not desirable.

Avoid stressed plants with stretched-out stems, yellow or brown leaves, or roots growing out of the bottom of the pot.

Forgo sickly clearance plants. They are not a bargain if they have withered, mushy, or disease-spotted leaves.

Choose firm bulbs, tubers, and rhizomes, not soft or dried-out ones.

Choose a shrub that is dense and well balanced.

Look for strong, upright leading shoots and a full crown on trees.

Maximize your budget

Get the best plants when you shop by following these tips:

Resist the urge to buy plants just because they are inexpensive or appealing.

Stick to a budget by shopping with a wish list and following a planting plan.

Shop cooperatively by buying bulbs in bulk and annuals in flats, for instance, and split them with other gardeners. Combine online or mail orders with friends to share shipping costs.

Research trees, shrubs, and other big purchases before you buy. Be aware of a plant's strengths and weaknesses before you add it to your garden and prevent costly mistakes.

Buy trees, shrubs, and perennials deeply discounted in late summer. The plants still have time to settle into the garden and root before winter. But there is a trade-off: Nurseries usually sell plants as-is at the end of the season with no guarantee.

Shop new varieties, brand names, and collector's specimens, but be aware that they may come at a premium price. Prices for new varieties usually drop after a few years when supply catches up with demand.

SHOP SMART

Compare Plants Look for lush, vigorous plants at the nursery.

Overall Appearance Look for balanced top growth and root mass.

Inspect Plants Look under leaves and poke soil to check for insects.

Peek at Roots Look for smooth, pale roots.

Keep Tabs on Tags

Plant tags include information that helps you choose suitable plants. Read tags and note hardiness, potential size, needs for light and water, and other care advice.

Mix, Match, Buy

Put together eye-catching plant combinations in your shopping cart. Coordinate colors and textures, trying different groupings to get a look you like, such as sedge, hosta, and coralbells.

Is Bigger Better?

Plants in economical cell-packs or small pots ultimately provide plenty of flowerpower within a season or two. Larger plants give more impact sooner.

Spring Gardeners dream of spring, envisioning daffodils gleaming in the sun and streams of bluebells flowing across the yard.

Summer The season of long, hot days brings waves of flowers and produce as the garden reaches its peak of activity.

Fall The autumn garden transforms like a kaleidoscope of color. Gardeners get busy with long to-do lists.

Winter Ongoing snow cover works like a blanket, insulating ground from freeze-thaw cycles and bolstering plants' survivability in cold climates.

Understanding Zones

Climate affects how plants grow and how you garden. Make sure your plants are suited to your Zone for success.

What's your zone?

The climate in your area consists of different weather patterns: temperature, wind, sunlight, frost, rain, snow, and humidity. The effects of the climate on your garden are complex and different than gardens across states and beyond.

Gardeners have a love-hate relationship with weather; gardens don't grow without light, rain, and heat. In spring, the morning sun on a rain-soaked garden welcomes blooms. But in a summer drought, the sun is cruel when it leaves earth cracked, petals scorched, and leaves wilted.

Gardening where it isn't easy

Every gardener faces climate challenges. Some locations are inherently extreme. Savvy gardeners adapt and look for ways to overcome obstacles. Dry desert gardens require conservative water use and native plants. In cold-winter areas, mulch helps plants survive dramatic temperature swings of freeze-thaw cycles that can injure or destroy plants.

Gardeners know that we cannot change the weather, so we strive to understand, gauge, and prepare for it. We turn to high-tech weather wizards and data, hoping for insights that will help us help our plants. We check the rain gauge, keep an ear out for frost warnings, and figure out how to shield evergreens from drying winter winds.

In the end, the best tool for weather-conscious gardeners is a well-adjusted attitude. Sharpen your senses of awe, humor, and defiance: Know that weather is an ally and a threat, and don't let it dampen your gardening spirit.

What is a microclimate?

Every garden has opportunities and limitations within a range of climates and conditions.

Within your yard, unique pockets surface with features (buildings, large rock forms, mature tree groups) and elevations (hills, valleys, plains) that alter the effects of atmospheric conditions such as moisture and temperature. The climate in that area may be warmer or colder than surrounding areas.

Areas on the south and west sides of a house are typically warmer than consistently shaded areas exposed to wind. Fences, walls, and large rocks can protect plants from wind and radiate heat, creating sheltered spots. Paved surfaces (patios, driveways, sidewalks) can absorb heat during the day and radiate into the landscape, moderating nighttime temperatures. Balconies and rooftops are unique aerial microclimates subject to drying winds.

Every garden has limiting factors and opportunities with a range of climates and conditions. Getting to know your circumstances will help you discover optimal places for specific plants.

> **LOW-MAINTENANCE GARDENING TIP**
>
> ## FINDING MICROCLIMATES IN YOUR YARD
>
> Notice the places where children and pets most likely go—protected from wind. Do the plants there bloom earlier or later than other plants in the yard? Is it always sunny or shaded there? Is there an impermeable surface (driveway or sidewalk) next to the area that captures heat? These are signs of sheltered spots that may offer ideal conditions for particular plants.

opposite, top Suiting plants to place translates into minimal future maintenance. This rooftop garden holds climbing hydrangea, daylilies, and ornamental grasses.

CHAPTER TWO

Gearing Up

The right tools make any gardening task easier and more efficient.

Well-made tools will last for generations.

The Gardener's Toolbox

Most gardeners get by with a few basic tools, but an increasing array of options promises more efficiency.

Good tools are designed to help you tackle specific jobs efficiently and comfortably. As you become more familiar with what a tool can do, you'll find more uses for it. A multipurpose tool, such as a spade, handles various chores with equal effectiveness and earns its keep quickly.

It pays to get the best-quality implements that you can afford. Price doesn't always reflect quality, but there is often more cost than value in replacing cheap tools. If you keep tools handy and in good shape, they will serve you well for years.

The best tools for you

Ask any gardener, "What is your favorite tool?" Each answer varies because the choice is personal, based on the gardener's temperament and gardening style. Tool choices are guided by age, strength, flexibility, balance, and experience.

The right tool suits your size and weight as well as garden work load. A short shovel proves handy enough for a petite gardener who tucks in a few plants periodically, while a more burly digger with a large rocky plot is better off with an extra-sturdy shovel with a long solid-wood handle.

A few good hand tools will fill the need for most gardening situations. And anyone can save time and effort with a high-quality spade, a large-yet-lightweight watering can, and a durable wheelbarrow.

A continually expanding array of specialized implements promises greater efficiency. New generations of gas- and electric-powered tools offer speed and maneuverability. If you're unsure of a tool's efficacy, borrow or rent one for a trial run.

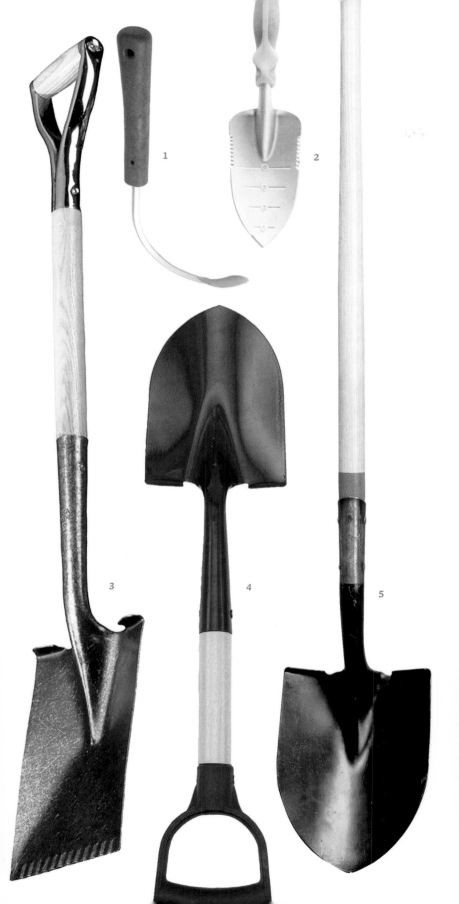

LOW-MAINTENANCE GARDENING TIP

BUY THE BEST TOOLS

Search online and in mail-order catalogs as well as at local nurseries for high-quality tools. Secondhand tools that have been well kept can be just as good as new ones.

DIGGING

Breaking ground and turning soil mark the rituals that bring plants to life.

1. HAND WEEDER The Cape Cod weeder shown works like a sharp bent finger and reaches into the tightest spots to dig out weeds. The best weeders are forged of steel and have sharp blades that pry, slice, or yank weeds out of the ground root and all. You'll find short- and long-handled weeders.

2. TROWEL Made to work as an extension of a gardener's hand, a good trowel digs small holes, cultivates soil, scoops soil into pots and amendments into planting holes, and pries out weeds. A longer handle provides greater leverage.

3. SPADE Most spades have a long flat rectangular blade with a straight profile and digging edge. Combined with a compact handle, blade precision lets you dig a perennial or shrub while keeping the root ball and surrounding soil intact. Use a spade to slice out planting holes, shape beds and borders, cut through sod, divide root masses, and break up soil.

4. SHORT SHOVEL The pint-size version of a shovel works like a giant trowel. It is well suited to smaller gardeners and those who prefer to work while kneeling or sitting.

5. SHOVEL Indispensable for digging, this versatile tool is also made to lift, carry, and throw soil, sand, gravel, compost, mulch, and such. The curved blade helps hold its load until you're ready to distribute the material.

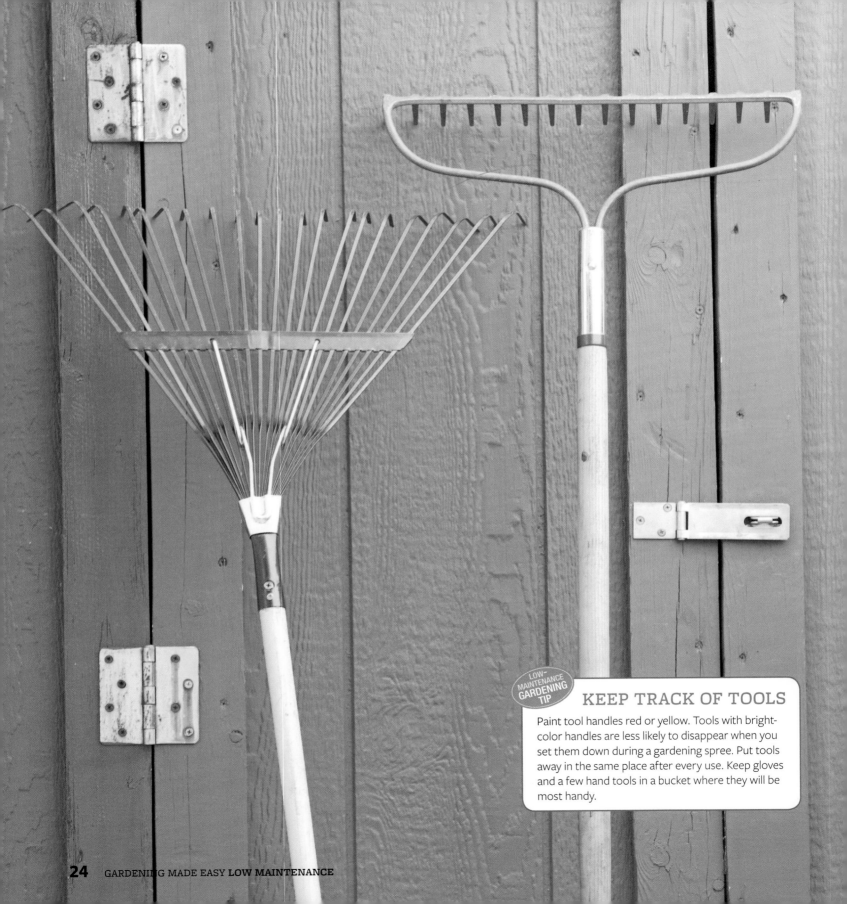

KEEP TRACK OF TOOLS

Paint tool handles red or yellow. Tools with bright-color handles are less likely to disappear when you set them down during a gardening spree. Put tools away in the same place after every use. Keep gloves and a few hand tools in a bucket where they will be most handy.

Cultivating

Get soil ready for planting by cultivating—using a tool to dig and turn over soil, stir it up, and break clumps into pieces.

Working soil is essential to prepare new beds or planting areas and removing weeds. Cultivating involves digging and turning soil. The process aerates the soil and makes it easier to plant. It also breaks up crusted soil surface and uproots weeds.

Various tools ease the laborious chores of loosening soil, making furrows for planting, mounding soil, mixing in an amendment or fertilizer, and even lifting weeds. A wide range of long- and short-handled tools features different blades for specific purposes—all can be categorized as cultivators. Beware: A tool shed can become overstocked quickly with cultivators. Basic ones include a garden rake, garden hoe, and hand cultivator.

Once soil has been tilled or turned over, refine with a hand cultivator of some sort. If you cultivate an area prior to planting, or work around widely spaced plants, you can cover more ground with a tool that has a wider head and more tines, such as a garden rake or garden fork.

LOW-MAINTENANCE GARDENING TIP

CULTIVATE YOUR GARDEN THE LOW-MAINTENANCE WAY

Prepare your garden for planting annuals or vegetables each year by turning the soil to loosen it. Work the soil when it is dry or damp—not wet—to avoid damaging soil structure.

opposite The strong, short metal tines of a garden rake (at right) level areas for planting. Pull and push the tool to cull clods and stones; flip it over and use the rake's flat backside to smooth soil. Use a flexible rake (far left) to clear leaves from lawn or garden areas or rake prunings into a pile.

above top Nothing beats a garden fork to loosen compacted soil and mix in compost. Forks with more than four tines lift and move loose materials, such as compost and mulch. **above bottom** A short-tined handheld fork allows you to work in the soil between plants without disturbing roots. **right** A basic hoe chops, grades, and weeds effectively. You may prefer another hoe with an angled, pointed, or swiveling blade and more refined uses.

25

REACH OUT

Tools with telescoping (extendable) handles provide extra reach to cut with minimal effort. A lightweight pole with nonslip grips eases strain on arms and hands.

LOW-MAINTENANCE GARDENING TIP

Cutting

Take the guesswork out of any cutting task: Start with the most-fitting tools.

Every time you cut a stem or branch of a plant, you prune it. Having the right tool that's sharp and up to the task is the first step in pruning successfully.

Choose a tool that fits in your hand so well you almost forget you're holding it. Hand shears should not open wider than your hand can extend comfortably. Find a left-handed tool if need be.

Also look for these features when choosing quality cutting tools: Well-cushioned and lightweight (aluminum or carbon composite) handles for comfortable use. Coated blades reduce friction, which keeps blades sharper and minimizes effort. Shock-absorbing cushion bumpers reduce fatigue. Replaceable steel blades are part of an ideal tool that can be taken apart for thorough cleaning. A safety latch that keeps the tool closed when not in use should be easy to flip with your thumb.

What you'll need

Outfit your tool box with three types of cutting tools: Hand pruners, loppers, and a pruning saw. If you have a hedge or lots of shrubs, add hedge shears to your collection.

You'll find two types of hand shears and may want to have both: Bypass pruners, the most indispensable cutting tool for gardeners, feature two precision-fit blades that slide past each other in scissorlike action. Anvil pruners pinch a branch between its straight blade and flat edge (anvil).

Pruning saws are the next step up from loppers, handling large-diameter branches. Most saws consist of a long blade with a handle at the end. The blade cuts on the pull stroke. The thicker the branch, the longer the blade should be and the fewer deeper teeth per inch it should have.

A CUT ABOVE

Sharp handheld cutting tools can make quick work of garden cleanup.

ANVIL PRUNERS are best for cutting deadwood branches up to ⅝ inch in diameter. Bypass pruners are best for making clean, close cuts on live stems up to 1 inch in diameter.

HEDGE SHEARS allow you to trim big and small twigs at the same time and produce a surface of dense, healthy growth. Choose an electric- or gas-powered version for large hedges or shrubs that must be trimmed frequently.

LOPPERS work the same as pruners, but the long handles provide the torque to slice cleanly through green branches. Use them to cut a branch up to 1½ inches in diameter in a single, firm motion. If this doesn't work, sharpen the blade or switch to a pruning saw.

opposite, far left Pole pruners feature a bypass pruner or saw head at the end of a long pole. Most extend to prune branches within a 12-foot reach and have changeable attachments. *opposite, above* A bow saw has a narrow blade that cuts on both push and pull strokes. Use it on branches narrower than the width of the bow. *opposite, middle* The handle of a straight saw provides a comfortable grip. This one has a sheath for storage. Its small teeth are best for hardwood or dead branches. *opposite, below* The design of a folding saw makes this tool convenient and safe. The molded handle is comfortable to hold. This one has large teeth for cutting green wood.

Holding and Hauling

Lighten loads and protect your back by using containers that are easy to fill, lift, carry, and empty.

Something always needs to be carried to or from the garden. When it comes to bulky or heavy loads, an efficient container helps. Try similar holders, such as a bucket, bushel basket, lidded bin and you'll likely find diverse uses for each. You'll need heavy-duty storage containers, for instance, which will keep birdseed and organic fertilizers away from mice. Opt for sturdiness over prettiness. Any good holder or hauler must endure rough use.

Wheelbarrow Balance a spacious container on a wheel or two, add a lever, and you have a nifty invention that functions deftly. Four wheels makes it a garden cart. Use either to tote many plants or rocks at once move loads of other heavy stuff, from compost to concrete.

Harvest basket Lightweight but strong, durable, and exceedingly portable, the best harvest basket or trug makes it easy to carry any garden pickings. A flat bottom makes the basket stable.

Tub A flexible plastic tub serves as the modern version of a bushel basket. This multipurpose container is equally able to hold soil or water, sticks or stones, fruit or flowers, tools or plants. It's also sturdy and washable.

Using Tools Properly

Tools are made with a specific task in mind. Your soil and garden type will dictate which tools you need and how to use them.

Most tools don't come with instruction manuals. Avoid accidents and damaged tools by using implements only for their intended purpose. If you use your spade as a pry bar, maybe it's time to get a pry bar.

Gardening tools have been designed and improved over the centuries through natural movements of users. Momentum powers most tools, but brute force often results in strain and pain. Every gardening tool has the potential to perform a job well without causing discomfort or injury as long as you use the tool correctly. Be aware of how to hold a tool as well as how to stand or sit when you use it. If you relax and enjoy the process of using tools properly, gardening can be more satisfying.

Take it easier

Gardening is an intense, whole-body activity. Ease into the season and avoid charging into chores to prevent injury. Avoid sore muscles by using your body and tools properly. Always use your legs and arms—not your back—to bear the brunt of any load. Bend your knees when lifting. Vary tasks, pace yourself, and take frequent breaks to minimize stiffness. During repetitive jobs, switch the tool from one hand or side of your body to the other.

opposite An adjustable pot lifter turns the chore of hoisting a hefty pot or rock into a quicker, easier task for two.

CAN YOU DIG IT?

Protect your back when digging, lifting, and taking on other weight-bearing chores.

RHYTHM IN MOTION The right way to lift: Bend at the knees and use your legs and arms—not your back—to lift a load. Scoop lighter loads to strike an efficient rhythm.

GET A GRIP Use short-handled tools for leverage tasks, such as scooping, scraping, and digging. Keep your grip light, letting the tool handle twist and turn, as you put your weight behind the push. Shift your weight with the movement of the tool.

ROCK AND ROLL Use long-handled tools for reaching tasks, such as raking and hoeing. A relaxed stance, with body bent over the tool, allows weight to shift and rock with the motion of the tool—forward and back—to power the dance.

Correct Digging Use a shovel appropriately by pushing the blade straight down into the soil. Keep your back upright and relaxed.

Use Your Weight Place a foot firmly on the shovel tread (flat or rolled edges at back of blade) and press down.

Garden Cleanup

The list of must-have tools for cleaning up the garden is short: willingness, elbow grease, and patience.

Cleaning the garden, especially at the beginning and end of the growing season, is essential to annual maintenance.

Early spring prompts gardeners to get out and pick up fallen branches and clear debris from beds. It's time to reach into beds with pruners in hand and cut back remaining old growth on plants before they get tangled in new growth.

Throughout the growing season, tidy for well-kept appearance. Regularly removing and disposing diseased, infested, or spent plant parts promotes a healthy garden.

Breaking a large cleanup job into smaller tasks will make it manageable and less overwhelming. Accomplish the mission in a weekend or two instead of pushing to finish in a day.

Autumn gold

The biggest cleaning job—dealing with autumn leaves—is necessary. Left on the lawn, whole leaves form a mat that can smother the grass and leave bare spots by next spring. Instead, put leaves to work for your lawn and garden.

Leaves contribute free organic material for composting and mulching. Shredding leaves with a mulching mower is a lot less work than raking and bagging. Plus, you can let the pieces fall. They will break down and feed the lawn. If you prefer, rake chopped or whole leaves into a pile where they can decompose over winter. Decayed leaves are beneficial for improving soil.

Your choice of tools can take the aches and blisters out of dealing with leaves. Use a rake with an ergonomic or padded handle, for instance.

LOW-MAINTENANCE GARDENING TIP

BASIC TOOLS ARE BEST

Reach for a simple set of tried-and-true tools rather than fancy high-tech gadgets for cleaning, watering, and other gardening activity. A few tools that serve various purposes will be used reliably over and over.

opposite, left New tools come along regularly with promises to make gardening easier. The Gardener's Hollow Leg, for example, is a strap-on holder that fulfills its potential as a hands-free bag for holding debris or harvest. **opposite, above** Pair a lawn or leaf rake with a large-capacity tip bag and you'll be ready for fall cleanup. Choose a wide, flexible-tine rake made of bamboo, plastic, or metal. **opposite, middle** The powerful airstream of a leaf blower clears a leaf-covered lawn swiftly. Use a gas- or electric-powered blower to clean areas that are difficult to reach with a rake. Wear ear plugs and safety goggles to protect ears and eyes. **opposite, below** At the end of the season, scrub pots with a stiff bristle brush to remove soil, mineral deposits, and stains. Clean pots promote healthy plants. Besides, you'll be ready to grow with clean pots next season.

CHAPTER THREE

Making Healthy Soil

One of the first lessons in low-maintenance gardening is starting with super soil.

Start at Ground Level

The secret to plant health and garden vitality is good soil.

Soil provides the first step to your garden's success. It really is that simple. Healthy soil holds enough water, air, and nutrients to sustain plant life and help it thrive. Healthy soil that teems with beneficial microorganisms holds the sun's warmth and nurtures helpful earthworms.

More than dirt

The soil of our Earth is not inert dirt but a balanced system of layers, from a foundation of bedrock to mineral-rich subsoil and living topsoil. In an endless spiral of life, plant and animal debris break down over time, enriching soil with organic material called humus.

Soil consists mostly of silt, sand, and clay particles plus organic matter, water, and air. The proportions of particles determine the type and texture of soil in your garden. There are thousands of kinds of soil that vary in composition. You may have rocky clay soil that is almost impossible to dig or cultivate. If you have the mucky clay soil found in some wet low-lying areas, it holds water and supports few crops.

In addition to sandy, silty, or clay soil, peaty soil contains mostly decomposed organic matter. It is acidic and tends to hold too much moisture and not enough nutrients. Chalky soil is stoney, dry, and alkaline; it needs improvement in order to support plant life.

Evaluating soil texture

Ideal soil or loam is a rich balance of humus, silt, sand, and clay. Dark, crumbly, and easy to work, loam is the goal of most gardeners.

Feel the soil by rubbing a pea-size bit between your fingers. Or smear a generous pinch of it on stone, paper, or the backside of a spade. The type and quality of your garden soil affects how much time you'll spend working to improve it.

Silty Soil Feels Coarse It is composed of minerals and organic material. Easy to work, it can hold moisture and nutrients, but compacts easily.

Clay Soil Feels Sticky This heavy stuff holds water and nutrients, but compacts easily and is difficult to work when dry. It turns slick when wet and sticks to a spade when you dig into it.

Sandy Soil Feels Gritty Sandy soil doesn't hold nutrients because it drains and dries out quickly. On the plus side: Sandy soil is easy to work.

LOW-MAINTENANCE GARDENING TIP

LIVING SOIL

Healthy soil teems with life, from easy-to-see earthworms and helpful insects to invisible microbes, such as beneficial fungi, nematodes, and bacteria. Apply compost annually to keep these microorganisms well fed.

opposite Turn over a shovelful of earth, then count: At least three or four earthworms indicate healthy soil.

Well-drained soil allows water to reach root zones, which makes for healthy plant growth. Add organic matter, such as compost and shredded leaves, to enrich the soil.

HELP SOIL DRAIN PROPERLY

If puddles remain a day or two after a soaking rain, the soil drains poorly. Grab a handful of soil and squeeze it. Well-draining soil crumbles as you squeeze. Sandy soil does not hold moisture and will feel gritty and dry.

Improving & Evaluating Soil

Nurturing soil is the best thing you can do for your garden to promote health and productivity.

Most soil falls short of the ideal—loose, rich in organic matter, and drainable—that is key to healthy plant growth. Adding organic materials, such as compost and shredded leaves, improves any soil.

Well-draining soil is another ideal. Drainage describes how water and air move through soil and plant root zones. In either too wet or too dry soil, plants grow poorly.

Adding organic matter to soil enhances its ability to soak up the water that plants need and drain away the excess. You can also improve drainage by building raised beds.

Contrary to common sense, adding sand to clay soil creates a concretelike result—the opposite of improved drainage. Instead, loosen soil by working in loads of organic matter.

Evaluating your soil

A soil analysis provides valuable information about your soil to help you improve it. If you've not had your soil tested, it's a worthwhile process. Before planting, go online or contact a local extension service or garden center for directions to submit a soil sample to a nearby laboratory. Home test kits are available online and at garden centers, but the generalized results have limited accuracy.

Laboratory analysis of soil comes at a small fee. The test will identify soil texture (proportions of sand, silt, and clay), nutrient content, and amount of organic matter. A soil test also reveals the pH level, which influences nutrient availability.

Once you know your soil components, you can amend the soil or choose plants adapted to the existing soil conditions. The analysis will suggest how to correct any nutrient deficiencies and adjust the pH.

EVALUATING SOIL

A soil analysis provides valuable information about your soil.

SOIL TESTING Even if you have gardened in the same place for years, a soil test will provide you with information that is not readily apparent. A test will take the guesswork out of fertilizing and amending soil.

WELCOME EARTHWORMS Organic matter attracts earthworms—nature's soil builders—into your garden. Earthworms turn organic matter into humus, adding their castings and boosting soil fertility. Their burrowing activity improves aeration and drainage. The more earthworms, the better the soil.

LOVE THAT LOAM When you improve the soil before planting, you make a smart investment that yields high returns in healthier, sturdier, easier-care plants.

Buying Soil

Plants depend on good soil for prosperity. Note that garden soil and potting soil or mixes differ and should not be used interchangeably.

Garden centers and landscape suppliers sell organic matter—including soils—in bags or bulk. Bagged products offer convenience, while bulk options prove more economical. Getting 2 or 3 cubic yards of compost (enough to fill a pickup truck) delivered for a new garden or other large project trades convenience for a small fee.

Packaged garden soil is specially designed to work in garden beds the same way potting mix works in pots. It typically includes a blend of topsoil, compost, and other amendments. You can usually count on it to be free of weed seeds.

When buying soil and soil amendments, it can be a challenge to determine how much you'll need for a project. These materials are usually sold by coverage (cubic feet or cubic yards) or by weight (pounds or tons). A ton of soil or sand may seem like too much, but it will fill up less than a cubic yard (27 cubic feet or a space 3 feet long, 3 feet wide, and 3 feet deep).

Potting soil and mixes

All potting mediums are not created equal. Container plants need porous soil that holds some moisture yet also drains well and is rich in nutrients. Garden soil is too heavy, compacts too easily, and drains poorly in containers. Experiment with potting soil mixes to discover which ones work best for your plants.

For potted plants outdoors or indoors, choose a fresh high-quality mix labeled with ingredients such as peat, vermiculite, and composted bark. The package will list whether it's a lightweight soilless mix (good for starting seeds) or an organic soil-based blend (good for growing herbs and other edibles). Potting soil alone is useful as the main ingredient in a mix, but some potting soils are nothing more than sterilized topsoil, which is too heavy for potted plants.

Premium specialty potting mixes ensure an appropriate balance of ingredients for optimum plant health. Some are blended specifically for a type of plant, such as cacti or African

Bag a Bargain Garden centers usually mark down and clear out bagged soil and amendments at the end of the garden season. They also discount damaged bags periodically that may have lost some contents.

Ready to Roll Save repeated trips to the garden center by stocking up on bagged topsoil, compost, and potting mix early in the garden season and have plenty on hand when you need it.

Perfect Mix A raised bed offers the opportunity to fill your garden with compost and peat moss for a nutrient-rich, well-draining mix.

USING THE BEST TOPSOIL

LOW-MAINTENANCE GARDENING TIP

Read the product label for bagged potting soil and look for ingredients such as compost and composted leaves. If possible, look for a dry, screened soil that does not contain debris. If the package does not list ingredients, how can you be sure what you're buying? Call the manufacturer and inquire.

POTTING MIX PRIMER

Container garden is easy when you use the right soil for your plants.

DESERTLIKE POTTING MIX Purchase a ready-made soil mix designed for cacti and succulents that provides porous, easily draining conditions. Or mix the soil yourself, using equal parts sand, perlite, and potting soil.

PREMIUM POTTING MIX Customize a potting mix by amending potting soil or pay for a premium product that has done the work for you. Added ingredients may include leaf mold, fertilizer, composted manure, and vermiculite or perlite.

ALL-PURPOSE POTTING MIX Read the product label for bagged potting mixes (and be aware of what you purchase) or make your own mix with peat, compost, perlite, and coarse sand.

violets. Other blends work for a particular purpose. A premium mix that contains slow-release fertilizer helps sustain long-term plantings such as shrubs and perennials. A mix that includes water-holding polymer crystals suits potted annuals and plants in hanging baskets.

Customize a potting mix by enriching it with compost, for instance. Improve the drainage with vermiculite. Or stir in polymer crystals to make a moisture-holding mix on the cheap.

How much soil or amendment will you buy?

A cubic yard of soil, compost, or mulch fills about this much space:

2 inches deep = 160 square feet

3 inches deep = 110 square feet

To figure cubic yards, consider a 10×20-foot garden = 200 square feet, for example. Multiply the area by .33 (one-third of a foot) to get cubic feet: 200 square feet × .33 = 66 cubic feet. Divide cubic feet by 27 to get cubic yards: 766 cubic feet / 27 = 2.5 cubic yards.

BLEND YOUR OWN

Make potting mix in a large pot or trash can with a lid that will also store the mix. Make a large batch for easy access to quick potting.

pH Factor & Working Soil

Soil pH is significant because it affects whether plants get essential nutrients. To have a good planting bed, you must work the soil. Make it easier by lifting and turning small loads of soil at a time.

Garden soil has a pH level that indicates acidity or alkalinity. Checking pH is done simply as part of a soil test or using an inexpensive tool from a garden center. Although plant preferences vary, most plants prefer a slightly acidic (6.5–7.0) pH.

Acid-loving plants include azalea, rhododendron, camellia, holly, and blueberry. Unless you live in a rainy region where the soil is typically acidic, you'll need to acidify the soil to help acid-loving plants thrive.

If soil is too acidic, add ground limestone from a garden center or hardware store.

If you live in a particularly dry region or a place with soils on top of limestone, soil will most likely be alkaline.

If soil is too alkaline, add powdered sulfur, iron sulfate, or an acidic fertilizer. Lower the pH over time by working in organic sources of acid, including pine needles or peat moss.

Working soil

The initial preparation of a garden is the biggest workout. Then routinely loosening soil before planting becomes easier each year as you continue to incorporate organic amendments in the process. Some gardeners dig by hand with a garden fork or spade. Others prefer to make the job easier using a power tiller.

Work soil only when it is damp. Soil is workable when you squeeze a handful and it forms a clump that breaks apart when poked. When soil is wet, let it dry out before digging.

Compacting soil

Working wet soil compacts it and causes rock-hard clods that will be difficult to break up. No matter how good the soil, if you subject it to traffic—by people, pets, or vehicles—it will become compacted. In compacted soil, plant roots won't get the air and water they need. Compaction is probably the most common soil ailment that you can prevent by avoiding walking and standing on wet beds and lawn.

Testing, Testing A pH soil meter or test kit, available from most garden suppliers, gives you a quick and accurate reading of your soil's pH level. Both methods measure pH on a scale from zero to 14, with 7 being neutral. Above 7 indicates alkaline soil; below 7 is acidic.

Acidify Soil Blueberry plants grow best in acidic soil (pH of 5 to 6). The plants benefit from regular soil amendments of pine needles, peat moss, or soil acidifier. These additions make the soil more acidic as they decompose.

WHAT ARE MICRONUTRIENTS?

Plants need at least 16 micronutrients or elements for healthy growth. Only four of them are commonly applied as fertilizers: nitrogen, phosphorus, potassium, and calcium. Plants also use large amounts of carbon, hydrogen, and oxygen (elements available in air and water) as well as sulfur and magnesium.

The elements needed in smaller quantities include iron, manganese, zinc, molybdenum, boron, and chlorine. These trace elements occur naturally in most soils, but in some regions, one or more of the micronutrients may be deficient.

You can add mineral-rich ground rock to soil to gradually increase its fertility. Ground limestone, gypsum, and rock phosphate, for example, add minerals to the soil over time. Organic fertilizers, such a greensand and bone meal, contain abundant micronutrients; most synthetic fertilizers do not.

TO TILL OR NOT TO TILL?
Compared to digging by hand, rototilling is a faster, easier method of preparing a large bed or renovating a lawn. Some say tilling causes soil compaction and upsets the balance of microorganisms and humus.

top If an area hasn't been worked much, prepare it for planting in spring when the soil is not too wet. Dig in with a garden fork and turn the soil. Break up any clods and level the surface. ***bottom*** If the area has been worked before, thrust the fork into the ground and rock the tool back and forth to loosen the soil. Work across the area, breaking up any clods. Remove stones.

left In order to do its work, any soil amendment must be mixed into the soil from 3 to 12 inches deep. **top** When amending areas among existing plantings with compost, work carefully to avoid injuring plant roots. **bottom** Mix in the amendment using a garden fork. Stab, rock, and stir up the soil to about 12 inches deep.

Amending

Add organic matter soil to promote the best conditions for plants.

For long-term success, it's better to feed the soil than the plants. Even good soil benefits from regular amendments. Organic amendments, such as shredded and rotted leaves (leaf mold) and peat moss, improve soil fertility along with its ability to hold and drain moisture. Inorganic materials, such as gypsum and limestone, improve soil structure and correct soil-mineral deficiencies.

Good soil nutrition

Improving soil is an ongoing process: Provide your garden soil with regular helpings of nourishing organic matter. Apply amendments individually or in combination at the beginning or end of the growing season or both. Also add amendments whenever you tuck in or remove plants. Add at least a 2-inch layer of compost or another organic amendment to your garden annually. In existing beds, amend open areas before plants leaf out.

Find what's available, depending on where you live. In coastal regions, seaweed and composted fish additives are easy to come by. In the Southwest, cotton burr compost is widely available; in the Northwest, mushroom compost; in the Northeast, salt marsh hay.

LOW-MAINTENANCE GARDENING TIP

HOW AMENDMENTS HELP SOIL

Amending soil with organic matter helps reduce compaction, making the soil easier to cultivate. Think of it as fluffing the soil, loosening it and incorporating air. These processes make it easier for plant roots to find air and water to grow.

AMENDING AN OPEN BED

1 LOADS OF GOODNESS
Improve the soil in a vacant bed by applying a 2-inch layer of compost or other amendment over the area.

2 ADD FERTILIZER, TOO
Apply fertilizer to counteract temporary nitrogen loss while uncomposted organic matter decomposes.

3 MIX WELL
Use a garden fork to incorporate amendments and fertilizer into the soil.

Amendments

Building healthy soil is an on-going process that will result in a healthy (and ultimately, low-maintenance!) garden.

Most gardens don't have already ideal soil. If your yard was the site of construction, it may miss topsoil, and the ground in your yard is either too sandy or claylike to support a successful garden or landscape. That's where soil amendments can save the day.

Upgrading soil

Healthy soil doesn't just happen. The ongoing addition of organic materials helps keep soil healthy and productive. Amendments not only change the nutrient value of soil; they also change the soil itself. Adding organic materials makes compacted soil loose to aid drainage, making soil easier to plant in (for you) and easier to grow in (for plants).

Although the soil in your garden may seem static, it is actually alive with microorganisms. Adding amendments helps it perform better.

Amendments should be added to soil before planting. You can till in amendments (in the case of a raised-bed garden) or add amendments to the soil in the planting hole (in the case of a tree or shrub).

If you have questions about which amendments are best for your yard, talk to experts at a garden center who are familiar with the soil in your area; they can suggest the best amendments for your soil and planting situation.

LET WORMS DO THE WORK

Red worms or wigglers turn vegetable waste into nutrient-rich humus, and this odorless stuff works efficiently when sprinkled into planting holes, seed rows, and pots. Castings improve soil fertility and drainage. The rich material also promotes plant health and vigor.

left The soil amendments you use will depend on what is readily available and practical. Try different amendments to see what works best for your garden.

ORGANIC SOIL AMENDMENTS

Turn to amendments whether you wish to generally improve soil or allay specific problems. Here are a sampling of soil amendments for your garden.

Leaf Mold Shredded and partially decomposed leaves lighten soil and promote healthy biological activity in soil. Not especially rich in nutrients, leaf mold often acidifies soil.

Compost Decomposed organic matter is free from a compost pile or commercial source. Made mostly from kitchen and yard waste, this premium soil conditioner adds nutrients that outperform fertilizers. It is the richest and best amendment of all.

Sphagnum Peat Moss This partially decomposed plant material soaks up water and nutrients like a sponge. It lightens and acidifies soil. Peat moss is a limited resource. Use coir, made from coconut husks, as an Earth-friendly alternative.

Composted Manure When well rotted and broken down, waste products of animals provide nitrogen and stabilize pH. It helps sandy soil retain moisture and loosens clay soil. Most manure comes from barnyard animals; cat and dog excrement is unsafe for garden use.

Vermiculite Flakes of mica (a mineral) expanded by heat absorb water, release it slowly, and keep container garden soil mix more porous.

Gypsum Add it to help leach salt out of soil. Add it to soil next to a street or sidewalk where plants suffer from winter salt applications. It can relieve aluminum toxicity and does not affect pH.

Coarse Sand Tiny rock particles can help open heavy soil and allow air to penetrate, but sand can also make clay soil worse. It's especially helpful for growing cactus, succulents, carrots, and asparagus.

Perlite These heat-expanded granules of volcanic ash do not absorb water but help potting soil drain and resist compaction.

left Nature's ideal plant food, finished compost, is dark and crumbly and feels like soil. It has a pleasant earthy aroma.
top You need only layer organic waste from the yard and kitchen in a pile. Sunshine, rain, and nature do the rest.
bottom A two-bin composting system allows you to make compost in one bin and keep a supply of finished compost in the other.

Making Compost

Turn yard debris and kitchen scraps into nature's ideal soil amendment.

Gardeners call it "black gold" with good reason. The luxuriously humus-rich organic material is the stuff that fuels legendary gardens. Compost amounts to free fertilizer.

Wherever you garden or whatever you grow, added compost improves the soil. In addition to making more air and water available to plants, compost slowly releases nutrients. It also helps protect plants from diseases and pests. Compost attracts earthworms and microorganisms that build soil.

Goodness grows

Composting is an easy way to go green and reduce your carbon footprint. You'll diminish your dependence on purchased fertilizers and amendments that require fossil fuels to make and distribute. Want to generate as much as one-third less garbage and save yourself from bagging all those leaves? You got it: Compost!

The easiest technique entails simply piling yard and kitchen waste in a designated place, with or without a bin. If you like, start a new pile when you begin to harvest compost from your first pile. By alternating the heap-harvest cycle with each pile, you'll have a continual source of compost. Whichever composting technique you use, continue adding materials when they're available.

Using a bin system or an open pile, you'll have finished compost in two to six months, depending on the weather. If you live in a freezing climate, you can continue to add to the pile over winter and let the debris break down as it will.

Expose a compost pile to the elements where some sun, rain, and other weather will help the decomposition process. But you can make compost indoors, too.

COMPOST ACTIVATOR

A commercial inoculant (dormant microorganisms) or soil activator is usually not necessary to make compost. A nitrogen source such as leaves or grass clippings is typically enough to initiate the process.

right Adding a compost layer around plants adds nutrients, holds moisture, and discourages weed growth.

Composting

Situate a compost bin or pile where it is most convenient for you.

Make your composting system simple or simpler. A bin, built or bought, encloses a compost pile and provides a tidy place to manage it. Numerous self-contained composting units are available to turn everyday stuff into garden gold.

Short on space? Keep a portable compost bin where it suits your lifestyle—on the back porch or in the kitchen, for instance. A bin allows compost to heat up and decompose faster. You'll find a variety of hard-working bins to help accomplish your mission.

Compost in something as unobtrusive as a plastic trash can by drilling air holes into it and cutting out the bottom. Partially bury it to put compost in contact with the earth to introduce beneficial microbes and earthworms.

Tips for successful composting

Get compost off to the best start possible and keep it going:

• Mix nitrogen-rich green materials (grass clippings, fresh garden debris, fruit and vegetable scraps, egg shells, coffee grounds, and tea bags) with carbon-loaded brown materials (chopped dry leaves and plant stalks, pine needles, small twigs, wood shavings, shredded newspaper). Try to compost about three times as many brown materials as green.

• Do not compost meat, bones, fat, dairy products, animal waste, branches, diseased plants, weeds with seed heads, and plants treated with herbicides or pesticides.

• Keep adding kitchen scraps to a compost pile over the winter in cold climates. They'll decompose as temperatures rise.

Kitchen Scraps This includes veggie and fruit waste, coffee grounds, tea bags, and eggshells.

Leaves and Twigs Chopped materials break down faster.

Grass Clippings Gather them as you mow, or rake afterwards.

Soil Starting a pile with a bit of soil introduces good bugs— the decomposers.

Yard Waste Leave out any diseased plant materials. Include small twigs.

KEEP COMPOST FRESH

Healthy compost smells like damp earth. If a smell arises from compost, it's a sign that the pile needs more air. Add dry leaves, twigs, or wood chips to the pile and turn it to incorporate the added carbon-rich material and air.

• When nature doesn't precipitate essential moisture for your compost pile, water it using a garden hose.

• Turning a compost pile annually promotes decomposition, but is not necessary.

• Although unusual, odor in a compost pile may indicate a lack of aeration. Turn the pile and add dry brown materials to increase air spaces.

• You can add a limited amount of fireplace ashes to a compost pile no more than once a year. Ashes are highly alkaline and can change pH rapidly. Do not compost ash from a charcoal grill.

• When starting a compost pile, include a few shovelfuls of garden soil. The microbes in the soil will fire up the decomposition process. Compost activating products are unnecessary.

• If you don't have space for a compost pile or leaf bin, compost leaves in bags available for municipal composting or yard waste programs.

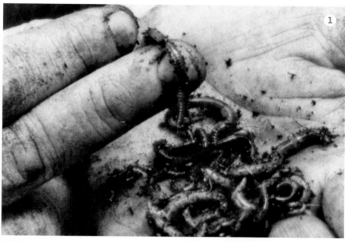

COMPOST YOUR OWN WAY
You can make compost in a variety of ways.

1. RED WIGGLERS These small red worms turn organic materials such as kitchen scraps into compost. Worm composting, or vermicomposting, in a plastic storage box is easy to do indoors, outdoors, or even at the office.

2. STACKABLE COMPOSTER This unit allows you to add sections to it as materials pile up. The lid has air-catching vents.

3. WHEELED TUMBLER Keep it near the back door for convenient loading; roll it to the garden to unload ready compost. Rotating composters can finish compost in weeks.

4. KITCHEN COMPOSTER This motorized appliance works quietly indoors to compost kitchen waste quickly. It tumbles and heats the materials in the process.

5. COMPOST BUCKET Collect kitchen scraps in a lidded container and store it handily on the counter or under the sink. When it is full of food scraps, take the bucket outdoors and empty it on the compost pile.

CHAPTER FOUR

Planning for Easy Care

Create beds and edging the easy way.
Organizing garden space reduces care.

Making a Garden Bed

Think low maintenance when adding a new bed. Transform an uncultivated area with no digging.

If the designated area for a new bed or border is covered with lawn, other groundcover, or weeds, you'll need to clear the area and prepare it for planting. Although there are several ways to accomplish this, one of the easiest methods harnesses sun, weather, and earthworms to turn turf into plantable earth

When making a new bed and determining its size, keep in mind that any length will do, but limit the width to 3 or 4 feet across. This width enables you to reach the center of the bed from either side. If you make the bed wider than 4 feet, place a path or stepping stones near the center of the bed so you can step across the garden without compacting the soil.

LOW-MAINTENANCE GARDENING TIP

PLANTING IMMEDIATELY IN A NEW NO-DIG BED

You can plant in a bed recently made on existing turf by cutting through the layers of paper and turf to make planting holes. Otherwise, wait 6 months until the cardboard and turf decompose.

1 STAKE OUT
First mow as close to the ground as possible. Then outline the new border or bed using stakes and landscape tape. Adjust the size and outline of the bed as desired.

2 SMOTHER TURF
Cover the area with cardboard or a 6- to 12-sheet layer of newspaper. Saturate the paper using a garden hose. Moisture promotes decomposition and draws earthworms to help the process. The paper will break down and add organic material to the soil.

3 LAYER COMPOST
Spread a 4- to 6-inch layer of compost on top of the paper. If you don't have enough compost, supplement it with high-quality topsoil or composted manure. Let the sun, weather, and earthworms work to decompose the layers.

4 BE PATIENT
The layers will decompose completely within about 6 months. You can make a bed like this one in fall and it will be ready for planting by spring, for example.

opposite: When you use a garden hose to lay out an irregular-shape planting bed, you can easily adjust size and shape.

Converting Lawn into Garden

As with any new garden, first determine a shape. Allow plenty of time to complete this job, breaking it into small tasks.

This time-tested conventional method for clearing turf involves digging and lifting sod to remove it, then digging compost into the soil to improve it. All told, it's a good workout.

Adding compost is essential when an area has been lawn for some time; soil needs nourishing. Ease the task of removing the sod by using a mechanical sod cutter, available at rental centers. Use a sod cutter to clear a large garden space in a small amount of time.

If the sod is good quality and not infested with weeds, save and replant it elsewhere. Once the sod is lifted, transplant it onto a bare area of your yard or share it with a neighbor. Otherwise, compost the sod.

Another way to get rid of turf

Some gardeners use herbicide to kill the aboveground portion of turf and weeds. Nonselective herbicides such as those containing glyphosate may be applied almost any time the turf and weeds are growing, and they work within a few weeks. To eradicate perennial weeds, spray plants in late fall when the herbicide will most readily kill the underground portion of the plants.

Kill Turf
Spray the herbicide precisely as directed on the product label. Never spray on a windy day.

Dig In
Dig and turn the dead grass into the new bed. Over time, the remains of the turf will deteriorate and add organic matter to the soil.

CLEARING TURF FOR A NEW BED

1 MARK THE PERIMETER
Outline the bed using chalk or flour. Use a spade to cut through the sod. Remove sections of sod, sliding a spade an inch or two below the roots of the turf.

2 REMOVE THE SOD
Using the spade to cut the sod again, slice off a section that you can easily lift. Transplant sod by laying it on open ground, tamping the sod into place with your foot, and watering the area thoroughly.

3 CLEAR THE AREA
As you remove the turf, also dig up any weeds or other groundcovers to clear the area. Spread a 3- to 6-inch layer of compost over the cleared area and dig it into the soil.

4 SMOOTH THE AREA
Work methodically over the area until the amendment is well cultivated. Break up any clods and remove any stones and other debris as you level the area.

MULTIPLE BEDS

Raised beds lend themselves to creative configurations. Build beds side by side, make some deeper than others, form a grid of beds, leave a path between them, or whatever your site and imagination suggest. Adjust dimensions and materials to customize your design.

Making a Raised Bed

Save time and effort with another simple method for creating a new planting area. Raised beds solve common garden problems and bring benefits.

Frame a bed with rot-resistant wood (cedar, cypress, or pressure-treated), stone, or concrete block. The frame prevents grass and weeds from creeping into the bed, resulting in less maintenance. Make a raised bed any size—a kit (available from mail order or online sources) simplifies the process. A 4×4-foot bed is perfect for a patio or other small space and easily accessible from any sides. If you have room, create a grid of raised beds with paths in between.

Benefits of raised beds

Raised beds dry out faster than conventional ones, so make yours at least 12 inches deep and customize it with drip irrigation; this watering technique delivers water directly to plant roots. Beds elevated 24 inches or more eliminate bending and stooping.

A raised bed provides a solution to poor soil, such as clay or bedrock. Fill your raised bed with an ideal mix of compost, topsoil, and composted manure for guaranteed good drainage. Avoid stepping on the soil and compacting it. After planting, spread a 2-inch layer of mulch such as chopped leaves or cocoa shells to help preserve soil moisture.

Raised beds offer a wealth of other benefits, too. Soil warms earlier in spring for a head start on the growing season. The frame provides a place to sit, kneel, or stand and makes gardening reachable. Raised beds offer affordable options, especially if you use recycled materials, such as concrete blocks for framing.

opposite Raised beds are ideal for harvestable crops, such as vegetables and herbs.

HOW TO MAKE A RAISED BED

1 LAY OUT
To make a two-tier bed, cut 10 pieces of 1×4 lumber to 4-foot lengths. Lay the boards in place to preview the bed.

2 ADD COLOR
Apply a premium water-base outdoor stain to enhance appearance and help blend the structure into the surroundings. This step is optional.

3 FASTEN CORNERS
Connect the boards using six metal corner brackets, stainless steel screws, and four inline connectors (available in a kit from a garden supply company).

4 LEVEL BED
Adjust the frame with shims if needed. Secure the frame using stakes included in the corner bracket kit and cover with plastic caps (also in the kit).

5 EXCAVATE SOD
Unless the ground is already prepared, dig to a depth of 6 inches to make room for root growth. Remove sod from the shallower front tier; turn over sod in the deeper back tier.

6 ADD SOIL
Fill beds with a good blend of two parts topsoil or garden soil and one part each mushroom compost, peat moss, and composted manure. Mix well before planting.

LOW-MAINTENANCE GARDENING TIP

PICK A TIME TO ADD A RAISED BED

Make a new bed in spring when the threat of frost has passed, then plant as soon as the bed is ready. Or make the new bed in fall, let the soil weather over winter, then plant as soon as weather allows.

Edging a Garden

A supreme multitasker, edging works hard to make a gardener's life a little easier.

Edging has a place in any garden. As a decorative element, it complements plantings and enhances your garden style. On the practical side, it keeps garden soil and mulch in, turf and weeds out.

You'll find a range of edging materials and designs. Widely used—if not the most attractive—prefabricated composite bender board or rimmed plastic gets the job done. Designed to be partially buried, both options can pop out of the ground.

Use your imagination to come up with prettier edging. Stones, recycled glass bottles, or bent green-wood branches can be repurposed at garden edges. Quality edging is made to withstand the elements. Most edging works whether your garden is framed by lawn or a hard surface, such as a sidewalk or driveway.

Edging buried part way in the ground should be particularly resistant to moisture. Edging made of wood or metal can be well-made and sturdy, but it won't last forever. Bricks or stones cost more than plastic or metal edging and they last longer.

A gravel edge makes an ideal mowing strip as well as a design element by emphasizing the creative curve of this bed.

LOW-MAINTENANCE GARDENING TIP

SHAPELY BEDS

Edging retains a garden bed shape. Whether edging is set flush with the ground or raised, it can take a straight or curved course. The length of an edger affects the shape of the curve. It's easier to lay smooth curves with short edgers and straight courses with long edgers.

GETTING AN EDGE

Garden edging delineates turf and garden or path and garden. Edging can be crisp and neat or casual, depending on taste and style.

Cutting Edge Carve a neat edge in minutes using a half-moon edger, spade, or power edger. Among the simplest of edges, this option is effective at keeping lawn and garden separate.

Down and Durable Bricks or pavers form a curved or straight edge that can be laid in various patterns. This version includes a strip to make mowing easier.

Living on the Edge Compact and low-growing plants, such as sweet alyssum 'Snow Princess', form ideal edging—easy care, budget-friendly, and quickly replaceable.

Casual Charm When you finish pruning trees and shrubs, transform the woody trimmings into a wattle, a simply woven traditional edging.

Pretty and Practical Scalloped concrete edging (5×12 inches) is inexpensive and easy to install. It provides a neat decorative edge along a walkway.

Double Duty Drip irrigation hides readily inside round-edged plastic edging. When the tubing is punctured, a drip emitter fits right into the edging and completes this creative approach to watering.

LOW-MAINTENANCE GARDENING TIP

USE STONE TO EDGE YOUR GARDEN

Tumbled fieldstone enhances a casual garden in a rustic setting. Uniform-cut stone, laid end to end, makes a tidy statement with a clearly defined sense of formal organization. Stone color may complement or contrast a setting.

Making a Mowing Strip

This quick, inexpensive, and satisfying project neatens garden appearance and saves time mowing and trimming around the garden.

A 4- to 12-inch-wide strip, laid just above ground level between the edge of a garden and lawn, makes mowing more efficient. Mower wheels roll over the strip while the blade cuts freely without nicking any edging. No additional trimming needed. As a bonus, a mowing strip also keeps turf and weeds from creeping into the bed.

When preparing the area between the lawn and garden for a mowing strip, clear an area wide enough to accommodate the mowing strip material you choose.

Mowing strip options

Concrete pavers are available in several colors, including gray, terra-cotta, and brown. Also find them in various shapes and sizes—all excellent for mowing strips. Or choose another edging material that suits your garden or expresses your personality. Consider these materials for a mowing strip: brick, concrete, flagstone, and recycled rubber edging.

> **LOW-MAINTENANCE GARDENING TIP**
>
> ## LAY A MOWING STRIP WITHOUT ADDING PAVERS OR BRICKS
>
> Excavate the area and leave the ground bare. You may need to weed the strip periodically or rein in garden plants that creep into the area.

HOW TO MAKE A MOWING STRIP

1 BEFORE
This garden will benefit from a mowing strip because its undefined edge merges with adjacent lawn. In the process of mowing, plants along the garden edge can be damaged

2 EXCAVATE
Use a spade to cut through the turf and form a crisp, well-defined edge. Clear a 5-inch-wide area between the garden and the lawn, removing any grass rhizomes and weeds, then loosening the soil.

3 LAY PAVERS
Place edgers end to end along the edge of the bed. Snuggle the pavers into place until they lie flat, about an inch above the soil surface. Remove any excess soil and toss it into the garden.

4 AFTER
Once all the pavers have been set, use a mallet to tamp each one into place just above ground level. You'll spend less time mowing and trimming around the garden.

opposite A brick mowing strip delineates between lawn and garden, and presents a road for mower wheels. You get a quick and clean edge without having to use a hand-edging tool.

Making an Internal Garden Path

Create a simple path through wide garden beds and borders to allow easy access to care for plants.

Large garden beds are beautiful to behold, but difficult to work in when wider than three feet across. How ever low-care your beds, you will need access to the interior for activities such as mulching, removing perennial plants for division, pruning, and replanting. That's where a small interior path comes in.

If you have a short distance to step, such as across the depth of a garden bed, a few well-placed stepping-stones will provide access to areas of the garden that you cannot easily reach from an outer edge. In addition, a path enables you to get from one side of the garden to the other without trampling plants or compacting soil, and it offers sure footing and a place to set tools or a harvest basket. In a large garden, make the path wide enough to accommodate a wheelbarrow.

A garden path is an easy addition with concrete stepping-stones from a garden center. If you like a rustic or natural look, source stones from a nursery; make sure they are flat on both sides for solid footing.

STEPS TO SUCCESS

1 SELECT MATERIALS
Round up newspaper, bark mulch, and concrete pavers or stepping-stones (one stepper for every 2½ feet of path). This 4-foot-wide path includes two steppers.

2 USE PAPER
Lay out the pathway using newspaper. Overlap the sheets of newspaper and layer them 6 to 10 deep. The paper will disintegrate eventually.

3 USE MULCH
Spread a 3-inch layer of bark mulch on the newspaper. Over time this organic mulch will break down and will need to be replaced.

4 ADD PAVERS
Take a walk across the path. Watch where your feet land as you stride. Those are the spots to place the pavers or stepping-stones.

opposite A garden pathway allows you to step in easily to mulch or weed without standing on existing plants. On flat ground, you can simply set stepping-stones on the ground. If the ground isn't level, inset the stones into the ground for better traction.

Choosing the Right Lawn

Whether you install a new lawn or care for an existing one, growing the right grass in the right place is essential.

Selecting appropriate grasses makes a lawn easier to maintain. How do you select the best grasses for your lawn? Narrow your choices depending on climate.

Lawns usually contain combinations of grass types, although some feature only one type of grass. Knowing which grasses will grow well in your yard helps determine how to care for the lawn and keep it in good shape. You get to decide whether to mow, feed, and water minimally—then relax in your hammock and admire your buffalograss.

Grasses might appear similar, but they vary in texture and growth rate. Grasses vary even more in terms of resistance to heat, cold, drought, shade, disease, and insects. Some tolerate heavy foot traffic; others won't spread into bare areas. It is useful to understand their differences.

Each variety of grass has strengths and weaknesses; there is no one best choice. Your grass selection also helps determine the best time to handle specific lawn care tasks. Check with your county extension service for recommended varieties suited to your location.

PLANT A NEW LAWN IN THE RIGHT SEASON

Plant warm-season grasses between spring and early summer. Plant cool-season grasses in late summer, early fall, or spring. Seed only fresh, high-quality seed. Prepackaged mixes are formulated for specific regions.

TURFGRASS CLIMATE MAP

Cool-season grasses grow best in the cool temperatures of spring and fall, and northern regions.

Warm-season grasses are best adapted to southern regions. They grow well during hot weather and become dormant and brown during cold weather.

Transition grasses, such as tall fescue, can tough it out in regions with hot summers and cold winters.

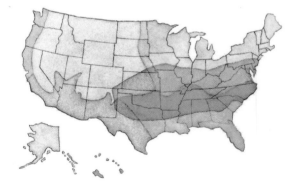

EASY-CARE GRASS
Select grasses suited to the conditions: sun or shade, dry or damp, high traffic or hillside. Less-vigorous grasses require less mowing yet recover slower from heavy traffic or play.

COOL-SEASON TURFGRASSES

Cool-season grasses are generally adapted to northern climates, where they grow vigorously in spring and fall and may turn brown in very hot summers.

Fine Fescue Good for shade, these wispy grass species need little maintenance. In mixes: hard, sheep, and chewings fescues suit dry areas; red fescue suits cool, wet regions of transition regions. Zones 4–8.

Kentucky Bluegrass Popular for cold hardiness, fine texture, and dark color, bluegrass does not withstand heavy foot traffic or shade. It needs more mowing, watering and fertilizing than other cool-season varieties. Zones 3–7.

Perennial Ryegrass This quick-growing, wear-resistant lawn suits transition regions. Ryegrass is fine-textured and dark green with a distinguishing sheen. It has little tolerance for severe winters and drought. Zones 3–7.

Tall Fescue Tolerant of drought, heat, shade, and pests, this coarse sturdy grass suits play and utility areas, especially in transition regions. Grow it as a single species, in a blend of tall fescue varieties, or mix with bluegrass. Zones 3–7.

WARM-SEASON TURFGRASSES

Warm-season grasses are adapted to the South, growing best in hot weather, then turning brown and going dormant when temperatures dip to freezing.

Centipedegrass A coarse slow-grower that needs less mowing and maintenance than many grasses. For light traffic areas and sandy soil. Zones 7–9.

Bermudagrass Vigorous and quick to recover from wear, it tolerates drought and salt, although it is intolerant of shade and prone to thatch. Zones 7–10.

St. Augustinegrass For a coarse but lush, thick lawn, this vigorous, tough grass tolerates some shade and salt but requires lots of upkeep. Zones 8–10.

Buffalograss This slow-growing native grass with fine blades needs no mowing. Drought and heat tolerant, it grows best in full sun. Zones 3–9.

Lawn Alternatives

If your lawn becomes too much work— too weedy, too weak, too needy—turn to groundcovers for reliable and low-maintenance replacements.

However hard you try to nurture a lawn, many yards have a place where grass grows poorly—under a tree in shade, on a slope, in a high-traffic area. Instead of wasting time and money trying to force grass to grow in unlikely places, turn to groundcovers, the problem-solving plants.

Easy-care groundcovers tame a slope, reduce erosion, and elbow out weeds. Their ability to creep and spread makes ground covers perfect plants for creating pathways alive with beautiful textures, colors, and blooms. Most creeping plants stand up to and provide lush carpets for outdoor rooms.

Pick your plants

Groundcovers include a vast array of plants, from low creepers to tall mounding options and even sprawling shrubs. The plants spread and sprawl by different means, whether creeping underground via roots and stems or by rooting branches and stems aboveground. Others grow in clumps, spreading wider each year.

Take advantage of the weedy nature of some plants and put them to work as groundcovers. But beware of introducing aggressive plants into your yard unless you take precautions. Install edging between groundcovers and lawn.

left top Carpet a shady spot with color. Magenta *Geranium macchorizum* 'Bevan's Variety' **left bottom** Bluestar creeper (*Isotoma fluviatilis*) makes a soft, resilient lawn and grows just about anywhere in Zones 5–9, even in clay soil.

PLANT EASY-CARE GROUNDCOVERS UNDER LARGE TREES

If grass grows poorly under a tree, first consider pruning a few of the tree's lower branches or thinning out the canopy to allow in more light. Replace the grass with a shade-tolerant groundcover, such as vinca or pachysandra.

PLANTS THAT KICK GRASS

The trick in using groundcovers successfully comes in selecting suitable plants for your garden. Native perennial groundcovers are good candidates. Nurseries and garden centers usually offer a range of groundcovers suited to the region—see what they recommend.

1. BUGLEWEED (*Ajuga*) This perennial features purplish-green, bronze, or variegated foliage and flowering spikes in spring; sun to light shade of Zones 3–9.

2. DICHONDRA (*D. micrantha*) This bright green or silver foliage works well in lawns instead of turfgrass in Zones 9–11. Mow, weed, feed, and water it regularly.

3. SPOTTED DEADNETTLE (*Lamium*) (Zones 4–8) This perennial sports variegated, aromatic leaves on 6-inch stems; blooms in white, pink, or lavender. It likes shade.

4. CORSICAN PEARLWORT (*Sagina subulata aurea*) Also known as Scotch moss, the perennial looks like moss and forms a chartreuse carpet in sun to light shade; Zones 4–7.

5. THYME (*Thymus*) Various forms, from creeping to bushing, as well as different colors, textures, and fragrances; grow in Zones 4–9.

6. STONECROP (*Sedum*) A range of perennial succulents from creeping to 4-inch-tall varieties for Zones 4–9. The plants need full sun and excellent drainage.

7. CREEPING VERONICA (*Veronica repens*) The 3-inch plant flowers in white to lavender in spring. Drought tolerant, it thrives in sun and heat; Zones 4–9. It can take foot traffic.

CHAPTER FIVE

Minimizing Garden Work

A low-maintenance plan makes gardening less time-consuming and labor-intensive.

left Large bark mulch works well for mulching trees and shrubs. Medium bark proves less slippery underfoot and makes a nice cover for a pathway. The texture of smaller bark suits perennial plants. **above** Dark-color mulches can help warm soil sooner in spring and prompt plant growth. **opposite** Tumbled stones add a decorative touch to a potted garden and preserve soil moisture.

Mulching: The Basics

Mulching is a time saver for you and a lifesaver for your plants. As a finishing touch, it neatens the garden to showcase the plants.

The process of spreading a thin, loose layer of shredded bark, chopped leaves, or other organic material over the soil between plants is nature's way of recycling. In forests, prairies, wetlands, and hedgerows, the process works the same as it does in gardens: A layer of mulch controls weeds, conserves soil moisture, insulates soil and plant roots from extreme temperatures, prevents erosion, and attracts earthworms.

A diverse array of mulches—homemade and commercial—includes organic options (compost, grass clippings, nutshells, pine needles) that break down and gradually add nutrients to the soil and improve its structure. Ornamental or inorganic mulches (shells, recycled glass, sheet plastic) are long-lasting and effective as well as decorative.

Mulch provides the ultimate multitasking materials for gardens, including beds and containers. Although mulch doesn't eliminate weeding, it slows the growth of weed seeds already present in soil and blocks new ones from entering. In the veggie garden, mulch cushions ripening produce, protecting it from rotting by sitting on damp soil. In containers, mulch deters squirrels, slugs, and other critters from pestering plantings.

Mulch isn't perfect

During periods of wet weather when mulch is piled too thickly, it can harbor too much moisture. As a result, the mulch can become matted or moldy. It may attract slugs, earwigs, and other eat-and-run insects that favor cool, moist, dark places. Straw and wood-based mulches deplete soil nitrogen temporarily after being applied.

PREVENT THE LOSS OF SOIL NITROGEN

The soil microbes that break down organic mulches compete with plants for nitrogen in soil. Plants show signs of nitrogen depletion in pale green or yellowing leaves or stunted growth. Minimize nitrogen loss that may occur when spreading wood or straw mulch by applying fertilizer first.

Types of Mulch

All mulches offer some benefits, but some have greater longevity; others excel aesthetically.

The majority of mulches are organic and decompose eventually. Chopped leaves break down quickly compared to large bark chunks, for example. Inorganic mulches such as sheet plastic and recycled glass do not decompose or add nutrients to soil, but they need replacing less often than organic options.

Your choice of mulch will depend on materials available in your region and where mulch will be applied. Coordinate the texture of mulch with the size and color of plants. Large bark mulch suits trees and shrubs, for example, while cocoa shell mulch works nicely in vegetable gardens.

When choosing mulch, consider practicalities, too. Lightweight mulches can migrate from a garden in a heavy rain or strong wind, especially when situated on a slope or exposed site. Select a mulch that's easy to walk on, sweep up, or mow over.

LOW-MAINTENANCE GARDENING TIP

MULCH MORE AND WEED LESS

A several-inch layer of mulch effectively smothers weed seeds, stopping them before they can grow in your garden. Mulching is a low-maintenance way to keep your garden and landscape weed-free. Plus, it helps retain soil moisture. It's a win-win.

Cocoa Shells Lightweight and dark brown, these hulls have a chocolaty aroma. They break down within a growing season. The material has been proven toxic to dogs.

Bark Chipped or shredded, mostly pine or fir nuggets decompose slowly. Barks can float and move in heavy rain. Use it in well-draining areas.

Grass Clippings
Collect them only if the lawn is overgrown and void of herbicide or other chemicals. Spread shallowly, clippings break down quickly and add nitrogen to soil.

Coir Another lightweight and porous option, ground coconut husk is especially effective at holding moisture. Sold in a compact compressed block.

Chopped Leaves Readily available, autumn leaves should be mowed over, shredded, or composted before using them as mulch. Whole leaves can blow away or mat down.

Gravel A permanent option for rock gardens, foundation plantings, paths, and places where other mulches present a fire risk in hot, dry climates, gravel also holds warmth.

Mushroom Compost Left after mushroom harvests, this fine, high-calcium compost conditions soil when incorporated at season's end, but not near acid-loving plants.

Pine Needles Creating the appearance of a forest floor, this fine-texture mulch gradually acidifies soil and works well for acid-loving plants, such as blueberries and azaleas.

Compost Dark and fine-textured, it blends readily with soil. Pile this free soil builder up to 4 inches deep on the garden annually.

Red Plastic Mulch This reflecting red film warms soil, retains moisture, and increases fruit production when used around tomato plants.

Recycled Glass Highly decorative and permanent, the tumbled glass conserves soil moisture. It adds sparkle and color to beds and containers.

Wood Shredded or chipped cedar and other woods fade over time and need to be replenished. Wood chips don't attract termites. Choose sustainable products.

When to Mulch and How Much

Timing varies depending on where you live and the type of plantings you plan to mulch. Buying and spreading mulch is a numbers game that takes into account varying factors.

Some gardeners keep their gardens mulched year-round as a weed-beating strategy. Permanent mulches, applied any time, need only occasional tidying. When topped off periodically with free mulch, wood-based products such as large bark chunks or cedar last and last.

In warm climates where gardening continues much of the year, mulch—or replenish mulch—as needed. Mulching at planting time is an efficient habit.

In cold climates, spring and fall mulching are typical. During the growing season, apply mulch in spring after established plants have emerged and new plantings are complete or in summer to suppress weeds, cool the soil, and reduce evaporation and the need to water.

Winter mulches are used in cold climates to insulate plant roots rather than to keep soil warm. Best applied after the ground freezes, winter mulch helps prevent damage to plants from freeze-thaw cycles. Spread too early, mulch can delay freezing of the ground, causing roots to go dormant later and possibly damaging them. You can apply an extra-thick (6- to 8-inch) winter blanket of straw on strawberries to protect plant crowns from freezing; then remove it in spring.

How much mulch?

When you're ready to buy mulch, get out your calculator. But don't worry. Buying mulch isn't complicated, and it presents an opportunity to save money. Although mulch quality and type vary, you don't need to pay top dollar to get the best mulch product.

Finding bargains

Look for inexpensive or free sources of mulch. Many communities gather and compost yard waste and offer it to gardeners at little or no cost. You may also find well-composted manure free for the hauling from a nearby farm or stable. In coastal areas where there's a fish-based industry, free fish-waste compost may be available. Find out how the material is composted or processed. If it is not turned, but sits and decomposes, you might take home compost laced with weed seeds and disease spores. In that case, the bargain is a problem in the making.

The cost of mulch varies, from homemade and free to permanent and costlier than most. Mulch sold in bulk is cheaper than bagged products. But if you don't have a vehicle for hauling bulk mulch, you'll have to pay a delivery fee, which can cancel out the savings. End-of-season sales make bagged mulch more economical. Store bagged mulch in a sheltered place or cover it well with a tarp to keep it dry over the winter.

By the numbers

How much mulch will you need to cover your garden? It depends on the type of mulch, the depth of coverage, and garden size. Most bagged mulch is sold by the cubic foot; bulk mulch by the cubic yard.

Picture a cubic foot as a box 1 foot tall, wide, and deep. For example, a 1-cubic-foot bag of mulch spread 3 inches deep will cover 4 square feet (12 inches divided by 3 inches equals 4). A 160-square-foot garden (8×20 feet) requires twenty 2-cubic-foot bags of mulch or fourteen 3-cubic-foot bags of mulch.

When purchasing mulch in bulk: To cover 1,000 square feet of garden with 2 inches of mulch, you'll need about 6 cubic yards of mulch (two to three pickup loads or fifty-five 3-cubic-foot bags).

left Give the garden a finished, neat appearance that lasts throughout the growing season. In summer use a 2- to 3-inch layer of mulch. **above top** A 3- to 4-inch layer of mulch in autumn helps trees, shrubs, and perennials withstand winter extremes.
above bottom Stock up and reap savings on packaged mulch that typically goes on sale at the end of the gardening season.

How to Apply Mulch

Instead of dumping bags of mulch around plants, use it like any good tool—with care and knowledge—to make the most of it.

For most mulches and soils, start with a mulch layer 2 to 3 inches deep for the growing season. Where the soil is sandy and quick drying, go for the higher end of the range. Where the soil is heavy with clay and drains poorly, aim for the shallower depth. Rock or recycled glass works best if laid only 1 or 2 inches deep.

Thicker mulching does not increase benefits. Instead, it can lead to problems with plant rot, disease, and pests. If mulch breaks down quickly in your region's climate, it's better to apply two thin layers over a year than one thick layer at once.

MULCH AND INSECTS

Wood, stone, and any other kind of mulch may harbor insects that favor cool, damp, dark conditions. Research shows that wood mulches do not attract or promote termites. If you're concerned, keep mulch 2 or 3 feet away from your home's foundation.

left top Spread most mulches 2 to 3 inches deep for the growing season. *left bottom* Steer clear of plant stems when spreading mulch. Pull mulch away from stems. *opposite* Use different mulches—one among plants and another for pathways—if you like, as long as they work and look well together.

Wait until after a rain or deeply water plants and feed them just before mulching. Sprinkle water on a dry mulch such as shredded wood after spreading it to prevent the material from wicking moisture away from plant roots.

When spreading mulch between plants, keep it several inches away from stems to prevent stems from rotting and to allow moisture to reach plant roots easily.

For winter, pile mulch 6 to 8 inches deep. If you use straw as a protective mulch for cool-season crops such as kale, use only clean straw free of weed seeds. A thick blanket of snow also provides an excellent winter mulch. When shoveling snow, it's okay to toss it on the garden to help keep plants covered.

LOW-MAINTENANCE GARDENING TIP
AVOID TOO MUCH OF A GOOD THING

Piled too deeply, mulch can hold excess moisture, prevent air penetration, and become sour and harm plants. Avoid piling mulch around a tree trunk, forming a volcano of sorts that can harbor rodents and insects, stress the tree, even kill it. Mulch wide—not deep—around trees.

MULCH MATTERS

Mulch is a low-maintenance miracle worker in the garden and containers.

NEW PLANTINGS Apply a 2- to 3-inch layer of mulch at planting time. Cover small plants with nursery pots to keep from burying them with mulch.

CONTAINER GARDEN Toss mulch between established plants, leaving a 1- to 2-inch layer well away from plant stems.

COOL-SEASON CROPS A 6- to 8-inch layer of clean straw helps insulate cool-season crops (cabbage) and soil from frost, extending the growing season.

TREES AND SHRUBS Spread shredded leaves over the root lines of trees and shrubs, keeping mulch a foot away from the trunk and beyond branch ends to cover the root zone.

BED EDGES Mulch helps keep bed edges neat and minimizes erosion. If mulch drifts into the lawn, push it back in place.

DECORATIVE EFFECT Use an inch of recycled glass or shells; 2 inches of an organic mulch in containers.

USE SLOW-RELEASE FERTILIZER

The granules or pellets are coated with a special resin and break down slowly in soil, releasing nutrients to plants over weeks or months, depending on the product. You will pay for the convenience.

Organic fertilizers, such as compost and rotted manure, release nutrients slowly and reduce the need for additional fertilizers.

Feeding: The Basics

Plants need various nutrients in order to grow and thrive. Most soils provide many of these essential nutrients. Fertilizers supply minerals that aren't always available adequately in soil.

Plants make their own food via photosynthesis. But when a gardener adds key nutrients to soil, it optimizes plant health and improves productivity. Nitrogen is needed for growth and green leaves. Phosphorous fuels strong roots. Potassium enhances flower and fruit formation and promotes disease resistance. Fertilizer labels indicate the percentage of the three key nutrients as a series of numbers, such as 15-30-15, which means that 15 percent of the product weight is nitrogen and potassium; 30 percent is phosphorous. The remainder consists of sand or other filler such as limestone.

Fertilizer replenishes the essential nutrients in soil and makes them available to plants. Plants have different nutrient requirements. Heavily blooming, sun-loving annuals require more feeding than foliage plants grown in shade, for example. It's up to you whether you fertilize your garden according to the specific recommendations of a soil test or follow a casual, plant-specific approach. Plants show signs of nutrient deficiency particularly in foliage, alerting gardeners to a need for fertilizer. Clues include pale or discolored leaves, weak or slow growth, and smaller leaves and flowers.

Plants also need micronutrients, including boron, chlorine, iron, and zinc. Unless a soil test indicates that manganese or another micronutrient is lacking, adding excess amounts can be toxic to plants.

Organic and synthetic fertilizers

Understanding the differences between the kinds of fertilizers, as well as what they can and cannot do, enables you to give your plants what they need for optimal health.

Organic fertilizers, made mostly from plants and animals, include compost, manure, fish emulsion, bone meal, kelp, cottonseed meal, alfalfa meal, and more. Organic fertilizers contain low levels of nutrients, but they improve soil structure, favor a healthy population of soil microbes and earthworms, and also contribute micronutrients that plants need. Some organic plant foods (chicken manure and fish emulsion) have odors that dissipate with time.

Synthetic fertilizers, made from petroleum and natural gas, offer convenient forms of specific formulations. The products require you to match their nutrient content to the needs of plants. Liquid fertilizer can give plants a quick boost.

Whether a fertilizer is formulated to be all-purpose (10-10-10) or plant-specific (a 4-12-4 starter solutions for seedlings and transplants, for example), organic or synthetic, each is made to promote healthy plants.

FORMS OF FERTILIZER

Narrow fertilizer options by choosing from two forms: dry and liquid. Although they're made for use in different situations, what matters most is that fertilizer must be dissolved to be of use to plants. You can make multiple applications of a soluble fertilizer or fewer applications of a less soluble one.

Liquid Food: Find liquid fertilizers in concentrated or premixed forms. Water-soluble foods (crystals or liquid concentrate) are mixed with water.

Dry Food: These fertilizers come in granules, powdery crystals, slow-release pellets, and spikes.

How to Apply Fertilizer

When it comes to nourishing plants of any kind, you'll find a wide selection of plant foods and methods to apply them in any garden or lawn situation as well as indoors.

Your goal when feeding is to ensure that the fertilizer is distributed evenly to plants. Liquid plant foods are absorbed quickly by roots. When using dry foods, scatter it over the soil surface between plants, keeping the fertilizer away from plant stems, then cultivate it into the soil. If dry fertilizer lands on plants it can burn them, so brush it off plants and into the soil. Always water after fertilizing if rain isn't on the horizon. Nutrients are water soluble, so good soil moisture is essential.

The frequency of feeding depends on plants, soil type, prevailing weather conditions, and type of fertilizer. Plants growing in pots or competing in close quarters need feeding more often. Organic fertilizers can be used less often than most synthetic fertilizers (other than slow-release ones). The best time to feed is in the growing season. Ease off plant food late in the season, when plant growth should be allowed to slow in preparation for winter.

Container gardens require consistent feeding because frequent watering flushes nutrients out of soil. Before potting plants, mix organic or time-release fertilizer into potting soil to make feeding easy. Then use liquid food to boost plants later on if need be.

Foliar fertilizer is an efficient means of feeding plants through leaves. A solution is sprayed on foliage and absorbed. It is an alternative to other liquid fertilizers.

left Use a hand fork to scratch in slow-release fertilizer. This time-release method of feeding offers nutrients all season.

AVOID OVERFEEDING

Don't be tempted to apply fertilizer at a higher rate than the product label recommends. There is no additional benefit to plants. Overfertilizing can injure plants and cause them to grow excessive foliage at the expense of flowers and fruit. If fertilizer is not used by plants or is spilled on an area near the garden, it will run off and pollute water supplies.

FERTILIZERS & APPLICATIONS

Whichever type of fertilizer or application you prefer, plants need to have the nutrients present in sufficient quantities and in a form they can use. Before buying fertilizer, read the package to understand formulations and directions for use. You'll find plant foods formulated for all plants, from acid-loving to roses, bulbs, and others. You can also give plants homemade fertilizers.

1. FERTILIZER SPIKES Tapped into the root zone soil at the base of a tree or shrub, fertilizer spikes dissolve slowly.

2. SIDE DRESSING Sprinkle granular fertilizer over the soil between plants, then scratch it into the soil, covering the granules.

3. ORGANIC SPIKE Nutrients move through potting mix rapidly. A spike dissolves slowly, feeding edible plants, such as tomato and basil.

4. BROADCAST GRANULES Cast dry fertilizer by hand or with a mechanical spreader, covering a lawn or other large area.

5. STARTER SOLUTION A specialty fertilizer for seedlings and transplants, the phosphorous-rich solution gives them a boost.

6. FOLIAR FEEDING A soluble fertilizer (fish emulsion) is diluted in water, sprayed on plant foliage, and absorbed by the leaves.

7. COMFREY TEA Make this nutrient-rich brew by steeping the large leaves of the herb in water, covered, for several days. Then use it as a liquid or foliar fertilizer.

8. FEEDING ANNUALS Water plants with soluble fertilizer every other week during the growing season if you like a routine—but avoid overfeeding in hopes of getting more flowers.

9. FEEDING BULBS Feed bulbs in spring to promote next year's flowers rather than adding bone meal at planting time, which invites squirrels to dig.

10. FEEDING ROSES Start the season giving roses a nutritious boost by working into soil alfalfa meal (nitrogen), banana peel (potassium), and Epsom salts (magnesium).

11. FEEDING INDOORS A fork works well for carefully mixing granular fertilizer into the soil of potted plants.

Watering: The Basics

Water is an essential element for all plants. But how do you know when a plant needs water? And how much water is enough?

Every plant needs water to survive and grow. Plants absorb water through roots and lose it through leaves. The process is affected by weather and soil as well as the plant type, size, and age and how you water.

Ideally, nature provides plants with sufficient rain, and the plants develop healthy root systems in well-draining soil. But with too much rain or poorly draining soil, plant roots can drown. If a hot, dry, or windy spell occurs and plants lose too much water, they wilt and may stop growing.

How much water

The need for water varies by plant species. Some plants require less water to survive and grow than others. And while some plants, such as cactus and succulents, can get by with minimal water, no plant can exist without some hydration.

WATER PLANTS THE RIGHT WAY

Water at the base of a plant, wetting the soil, not the foliage. The goal: Deliver water to the roots where it is needed.

left Avoid applying water faster than the soil can absorb it. A gentle, slow trickle seeps deeper, especially in dry soil. Unless applied carefully, water runs off extremely dry soil.

A good rule when it comes to watering is this: An inch of rain or supplemental water per week sustains most plants. Deep, thorough watering reaches the root zone, 6 to 12 inches deep, of most plants.

Deeper, less-frequent watering encourages plants to root more deeply, enabling them to better withstand drought. This goes for all kinds of plants, from those grown in containers to lawns. More-developed root systems are able to drink in moisture more effectively. Shallow, frequent watering does more harm than good: It promotes shallow root growth, making plants more vulnerable to damage from drought, weeds, and pests.

Timing of watering is as important as how you water. Watering early in the day is ideal because less moisture will be lost to evaporation. Also, if plant leaves get wet, light, heat, and wind will dry them and help prevent diseases, such as mildew, that thrive on moisture.

LOW-MAINTENANCE GARDENING TIP

AVOID GIVING TOO MUCH WATER

Overwatering is one of the most common causes of plant death. If the soil is continually saturated, plant roots cannot get enough air and they will rot. Too-wet soil feels wet to the touch. It may smell sour and—ironically—may cause plants to wilt. Add sand to soil to increase the drainage. Although some plants can tolerate (and even thrive) in moist soils, many will not. Read the plant label when you plant to determine the water requirements.

READ THE SIGNS

Use visual and tactile cues to determine the needs of your garden. Plants will guide you in their care if you look for symptoms of too little or too much.

NOT ENOUGH
Wilting in early morning or evening indicates a plant's immediate need for water. Some plants wilt in the heat of midday but recover by evening.

TOO MUCH
An overabundance of rain or too-generous watering can be as deadly as not enough moisture. If roots rot, plants die.

FEEL SOIL
Check soil for moisture by poking a finger into it, up to the first or second knuckle. If the soil feels dry, it's time to water.

READ RAIN GAUGE
Monitor weather reports or check the rain gauge, then water each week to make up for lack of rainfall.

Conserving Water

Water is among the most precious resources on the earth. In dry regions and areas prone to drought, water conservation is essential. Rain barrels are a tried-and-true practice to harvest free rainwater.

Many communities restrict water use for lawns and gardens, requiring conservation. Even if you live in a high-rainfall region, your plants may not receive adequate water at the right time. Conservation methods promote healthy plants that can cope with drought. Whether or not water is scarce where you garden, it pays to conserve—you'll see an appreciable difference in your water bill.

There are many effective ways to reduce water use yet have a beautiful productive garden. Some strategies involve a change of habits; others involve choices of equipment, plants, and other landscape features, including

Improve soil Adding loads of organic matter helps soil soak up water and stay moist longer.

Mulch Cover bare soil with a 2- to 3-inch layer of chopped leaves, bark, or compost.

Reduce lawn area Retain only what you use. Aerate the lawn annually. Use a mulching mower and recycle lawn clippings.

Use efficient watering methods Drip irrigation and soaker hoses lose less water to evaporation than sprinklers. Water only when needed, not automatically and regardless of weather.

Use free water Set a rain barrel under a downspout and collect rainwater.

How to save water with a rain barrel

One-half inch of rain yields 300 gallons of watershed from 1,000 square feet of roof. You only have to catch it. Once you realize how much water can be saved with one barrel, you'll want one at every downspout. A 40- to 60-gallon rain barrel under a downspout fills surprisingly quickly. It collects water free of chemicals, such as chlorine and fluoride, added to municipal water.

Rain barrel safety

Select a barrel that adapts for overflow, allowing you to direct excess rainwater away from the barrel (and home foundation) or to link multiple barrels together. Screen any opening to keep out debris and mosquitoes. Place a rain barrel on stable, level ground or on concrete pavers or gravel to prevent tipping and spilling.

COLLECT RAINWATER

Whether you purchase a ready-made rain barrel or make one, you can add a hose spigot near the base of the barrel for easy access to the stored water. Attach a garden hose to the spigot, if you like, to route the water to plants.

left Any place in your landscape that uses water has potential for conserving it. **opposite left** Attach a garden hose to a rain barrel via a spigot to route the water easily to plants. You can add a spigot to a purchased or homemade barrel. **opposite right top** Before winter arrives in cold climates, disconnect and empty a rain barrel. If water is left in the barrel, freeze-thaw cycles can damage it. **opposite right bottom** Mixed into potted gardens or beds, polymer crystals absorb water and release it into soil as needed.

Hand-Watering and Garden Hoses

Watering, like most garden tasks, is not a one-size-fits-all practice. There are plenty of ways to keep your garden green while using water efficiently.

Your choice of watering method depends on the plants you grow. Young or small plants and container gardens can be watered deftly by hand, using a hose or a watering can. A wave of a watering wand, attached to a hose, is often the best way to reach bedding plants and hanging baskets. It also helps you quench plants growing under eaves or other out-of-the-way places. The gentle shower from a can proves perfect for just-planted seeds and tiny seedlings. Why drag a bulky hose across the yard when a watering can lets you pick it up and go?

Hand-watering involves no soil preparation or equipment installation. It is more time consuming for the gardener and commonly leads to underwatering because most gardeners do not have the patience to water plants as long as needed.

When you step close enough to a plant to hand-water, you're also close enough to inspect its health, inhale its aroma, and appreciate its beauty.

Garden hoses

A dependable hose requires a lightweight yet flexible material that can handle water pressure and weather extremes. The best hoses consist of multiple layers, or plies, of rubber, vinyl, and reinforcing materials.

Large-diameter hoses deliver more water pressure and volume but weigh more than smaller ones. A ¾-inch hose delivers 65 percent more water than a ⅝-inch one.

Use a watering can with a gentle spray to water tender seedlings.

GARDEN HOSES

Look for various ways to make a hose do the work, from an efficient attachment to convenient storage.

Rubber Hose The best hoses bend easily without kinking. Brass fittings and high-quality metal (brass) attachments last years longer than inexpensive alternatives.

Coil Hose Especially useful for watering in a confined space, such as a greenhouse or balcony, the compact 25- to 50-foot hose won't tangle or require a storage reel.

Soaker Hose A porous or leaky hose sweats water, soaking ground up to 3 feet away. Burying the hose under mulch minimizes runoff and evaporation.

Water Wand Make watering efficient with a hose-end attachment. It may have a shut-off mechanism and spray adjustments from gentle shower to forceful stream.

Hose Storage A durable container conceals a garden hose and keeps it handy. A hole in the side of the container allows the hose to connect conveniently to a faucet.

Good Timing Use a programmable two-zone water timer that enables you to use one hose for drip irrigation at the same time as you use another hose for hand-watering.

CHOOSE A GOOD WATERING CAN

LOW-MAINTENANCE GARDENING TIP

A 2- to 3-gallon can holds as much water as most people can comfortably carry. Two-handled cans tilt easily with less hand and arm strain. A brass or galvanized rose (perforated spout attachment) offers longevity.

left Space tubing 12 to 24 inches apart in beds to wet soil yet promote root development. **above top** Water seeping into soil is difficult to see. After a watering cycle, use a trowel to check soil moisture. **above bottom** Control a watering system with a programmable timer, turning it on and off even when you're away.

Drip Irrigation

Good for any size garden and plants that need even moisture, a drip irrigation system applies water slowly and efficiently to specific areas.

A drip or microirrigation system saves money and water by delivering moisture to soil near plants with as little evaporation and runoff as possible. You'll save money by installing a system over a weekend or two, starting with a garden near a spigot.

Easy to install and adaptable to most gardens, drip systems can be purchased at hardware stores. You'll find kits that include emitters, tubing, and other components. Customize your system, adding emitters on lines to it.

First, sketch a plan. Measure the tubing length needed for a simple one-zone system. Count the type of emitters (dripper, sprayer, or sprinkler) and flow rate you will need, depending on plant needs. Match brands of tubing and emitters to avoid sizing issues.

Prevent problems

Attach a backflow prevention device to the spigot to prevent contaminated water from flowing into the water system. Also attach a filter to trap particles before they get into the system and clog emitters. Automate your system with a timer. Use a Y-splitter with shutoffs so you can use the drip system and a garden hose. Match hose thread or pipe thread when you buy parts. Check your system seasonally, especially in hard-water areas, to make sure the emitters and filter are not clogged, the lines and screens are not plugged, and the timer works.

LOW-MAINTENANCE GARDENING TIP

WATER CONTAINERS THE SMART WAY: DRIP IRRIGATION

Run a main supply line from a spigot to the vicinity of your containers. Connect each container to the main line with a branching line. Run the irrigation line up the back side of each container to hide the tubing.

AVOID WASTING WATER

An automatic timer allows you to decide how often and how long to deliver water to plants with a drip irrigation system. Override the timer during wet or cold weather. Turn off the system and drain the main line before freezing weather arrives.

1 SNAKE TUBING
Set tubing in sun to make it more bendable. Snake the line through the garden, then cut it to fit.

2 FLUSH LINE
Run water through the tubing to clear debris. Crimp and clamp the end.

3 INTERSECTION
Cut the line and insert a T-fitting to connect a branching line and run the system in another direction.

4 PUNCH HOLES
Use the kit tool to make a hole for each emitter connection. Use a "goof" plug to patch a hole.

5 ADD LINE
Plug thin, flexible tubing into the drip line. Place an emitter at the end of the tubing.

6 HOLD THE LINE
Use clips to hold the irrigation line in place. Use mulch to cover the line and conserve moisture.

Irrigation Tips

Underground sprinkler systems add convenience and the assurance that your valuable landscape plants and lawn will get the water they need when they need it.

Keep an in-ground sprinkler system working well with regular maintenance. Making occasional adjustments and repairs to the system will keep it working efficiently. As plants grow, seasons change, and equipment fails unexpectedly, you can handle simple problems, when you know how to identify them.

Monitor soil and plants regularly, checking for uniform irrigation. Adjust irrigation heads as plants grow and begin to block a spray pattern.

Always drain the system to prepare for winter in a freezing area. Standing water turns to ice in the pipes and can lead to major leaks and repairs. The water must be shut off, the lines drained, and the valves cleared. The process depends on whether you have a gravity drain or compressed-air system.

LOW-MAINTENANCE GARDENING TIP

ENJOY A DROUGHT-TOLERANT LAWN

Native turfgrasses and some other varieties have adapted to withstand drought and heat. Buffalograss, tall fescue, and sheep fescue are among those that need little water to thrive. Check with your extension service to identify drought-tolerant turfgrass varieties for your region.

---

left In-ground sprinkler heads pop up and water, then disappear in the lawn when done. **opposite** Sprinkler heads can be directed away from walkways.

Watering lawn

Portable or permanent sprinklers do the job. Choose the best system for your yard to supplement rainfall as needed.

Most people overwater lawns. Overwatering weakens plant roots, which provides an entrance for many diseases. Water a lawn deeply and infrequently. Water established lawn 1 inch every 7 to 14 days without rain. New lawn needs daily watering.

When water is scarce, during summer's peak, many turfgrasses go dormant (rest and stop growing). During a drought, it is better not to water at all than to water small amounts. Small amounts can prevent the lawn from resting and encourage weed growth. If you let a lawn go dormant, rest assured it will come back when rainfall and cooler weather return.

A portable sprinkler offers an inexpensive way to water occasionally. To cover a large area, move the sprinkler around. Be aware of sprinkler coverage area and pattern; compensate for uneven distribution.

In arid regions, an in-ground sprinkler system is an investment in maintaining lawn conveniently and efficiently. Even so, homes with a permanent system use more water than those without one.

WHEN TO CALL A PRO

LOW-MAINTENANCE GARDENING TIP

Turn to a qualified professional irrigation specialist when your efforts aren't improving the sprinkler system or you're not comfortable tackling a repair or maintenance. Not all repairs or maintenance tasks are do-it-yourself jobs.

TUNING UP IN-GROUND IRRIGATION

Check all the aspects of your irrigation system yearly to make sure it operates to its full potential.

CHECK CONTROL
Annually replace the backup battery in an automatic timer, following manufacturer directions.

PREVENT RUNOFF
If you consistently see runoff from your lawn or garden after irrigating, the system is running too long and needs adjusting.

CLOGGED NOZZLE
Fix low water flow or an uneven spray pattern by unscrewing the sprinkler head and rinsing the filter.

REALIGN SPRINKLER
Depending on the type of sprinkler head, adjust it to spray water in the direction you want.

CLEAR OBSTRUCTIONS
Trim plant foliage or turf away from a sprinkler to remove interference with its spray.

Waterwise Gardens

Wherever you live, the simplest way to use less water is obvious: Grow plants that use less water.

Creating a garden less dependent on water makes sense. You'll save money, time, and effort by taking simple steps toward a more self-sufficient garden.

Choose native plants. Plants adapted to your climate can cope with weather extremes. They may need water during severe drought.

Group plants with similar needs for water. Plant and irrigate in zones, with thirsty plants closer to the house, low-water plants farther away. Group containers to reduce evaporation from them.

Reduce lawn. It is the biggest user of water in most yards, on average. Retain only enough lawn for your needs. Replace lawn with drought-tolerant turfgrass or groundcovers.

Plant in late summer or early fall. Perennials, shrubs, and trees will need less water as they establish themselves before winter. As top growth slows with cooler weather, root growth will continue until the soil cools.

Shelter plants with a windbreak or added shade. Plants lose more water on sites exposed to wind or full sun.

Manage rainwater. A basin, swale, berm, or series of terraces can catch water and guide it to planting areas. Redirect downspouts to gardens, instead of letting rain run off the roof and down the street. Use permeable paving.

LOW-MAINTENANCE GARDENING TIP

PLANT NATIVES

Create a low-water garden with native plants that thrive in your region. The plant palette may be subtle or bold, as long as it includes regionally suitable plants that will thrive in both normal and dry years.

left Use a downspout attachment that directs harvested rainwater into planting areas. *opposite* Embrace a low-water landscape. Faced with dust and hot sun in summer, sand and salt in winter, this streetside garden features tough plants that withstand the challenges. Low-growing, drought-tolerant perennials do the trick.

ADD ROCKS TO A DRY GARDEN

Strategically placed rock groupings create a natural-looking setting. They also help direct rainwater, slowing it down so it soaks into the ground and reaches plants instead of running off soil. In addition, gravel works well as a moisture-preserving mulch.

Less-Thirsty Plants

In many places, water restrictions and drought have become an ongoing concern. Dealing with the situation starts by making appropriate plant choices.

Select plants that require minimal moisture to survive. Usually the plants most resistant to drought are natives of the region. Many shrubs and perennials have adapted to environments with hot and sunny conditions or prolonged dry spells. In addition to local nurseries, sources for drought-tolerant plants include mail-order suppliers.

Where water is scarce

Water shortages already affect a number of states, and that number will grow in the future. Learn about drought-tolerant plants and how to use them in the landscape so your garden is less water-dependent.

New plants are especially vulnerable to dry conditions. Most perennials need regular watering the first year to become established, but less water overall than annuals. Deep, infrequent watering encourages deep roots.

Artemisia The lacy foliage of silvery artemisia blends and softens colors. Some varieties can become invasive. Zones 5–8.

Catmint (*Nepeta racemosa*) The shrubby plants have fragrant blue-green foliage. The flowers beckon butterflies and hummingbirds in Zones 4–10.

False indigo (*Baptisia*) A long-lived North American native, it has tall flower spikes and attractive seedpods. Grow it in full to part sun. Zones 3–10.

Lamb's-ears (*Stachys byzantina*) Prized for its fuzzy silvery foliage, it forms a dense groundcover in full sun and well-draining soil. Zones 3–10.

Penstemon, pineleaf (*P. pinifolius*)
A Southwest native with needlelike evergreen leaves, it blooms from summer to fall in Zones 4–10.

Salvia, perennial
Plants vary from small perennials to large woody shrubs with sturdy foliage and long-season blooms in Zones 4–10.

Sedum, showy (*S. spectabile*) Upright succulents are clump-forming and handsome year-round; good companions for a range of other perennials in Zones 3–10.

Sundrops (*Oenothera*)
A fast-growing spreader with bright yellow flowers on sturdy, 18- to 24-inch stems. Grow in full to part sun in Zones 4–9.

Thyme, creeping (*Thymus praecox*)
This ground-hugging herb forms a dense evergreen mat. It flowers in late spring and early summer. Zones 4–10.

Tickseed (*Coreopsis*)
This low-maintenance, long-blooming tickseed needs well-draining soil and full sun. Zones 4–10.

Yarrow (*Achillea*)
Recognized for its ferny foliage and flat-topped flower clusters, its varieties boast season-long color in Zones 2–10.

Dianthus Old-fashioned favorites have grassy blue-green foliage and dainty clove-scented blooms. Plant in full sun. Zones 3–10.

Pruning: The Basics

Pruning is essential to plant health, beauty, and safety. Keep these priorities—and a few others—in mind when you prune.

Regular and corrective pruning keeps trees, shrubs, and woody vines healthy by eliminating some problems and preventing others. Generally, pruning encourages new growth and vigor. Removing select branches lets light and air reach more parts of the plant. The ongoing priorities of pruning are the same for any plant: Remove damaged, diseased, or dead parts. When left on the plant, these parts harbor pests and disease.

Prune with a purpose

Accomplish other goals with pruning, improving the plant one way or another. Pruning is necessary when limbs create a safety issue such as leaning precariously over a house or reaching overhead wires. When you wish to see more flowers or fruit on roses, raspberries, apples, camellias, or others, pruning is needed. Pruning also reveals colorful bark of trees, such as river birch and paperbark maple. And pruning prompts new colorful stems of shrubs, such as dogwood and kerria.

You can control a plant's size with good reason, whether you have a shrub planted too close to the house, an overly assertive vine, or a shapely topiary. Similarly, pruning maintains a plant's natural form or creates a formal shape. It depends on the plant and your goal, whether you have a casual hedge of lilacs or a tidy border of boxwoods.

In the long run, pruning preserves a plant's integrity and your investment in it. Trees, shrubs, and woody vines vary in their growth habits and needs for pruning. But pruning helps you get to know your plants and prompts them to become their best.

left top A good pair of pruners is an essential tool in the garden. A protective sheath allows you to carry them while you work. **left bottom** Use clean, sharp pruning tools for clean and healthy cuts.

Pruning safely

Pruning can be hazardous. Common sense and the proper use of the right equipment will keep you safe while pruning.

• Dress appropriately for pruning, wearing long pants, long-sleeved shirt, gloves, safety glasses, and nonskid shoes. A brimmed hat prevents sun from obscuring vision.

• Keep tools sharp and clean. Store a sharp tool in a protective sheath if possible. Always carry pruning tools with points facing down.

• Choose a clear, still, dry day to prune. Using loppers or pruners when windy is dangerous and ineffective.

• If you must prune from a stepladder, tie it securely to the tree. Keep one hand on the ladder and one hand on your pruning saw. Station someone on the ground to secure the ladder.

LOW-MAINTENANCE GARDENING TIP

PRUNE FOR IMPROVED GROWTH

Removing parts of a tree or shrub may feel counterintuitive for plants that you want to grow big and tall. But pruning actually stimulates growth. Include seasonal pruning in your yearly gardening regimen. Concentrate on pruning basics and let the plant do the rest. Watch for results of your cuts, and pruning will become a pleasure as you gain confidence.

WHEN TO CUT

In addition to regular pruning, removing dead or damaged growth will keep plants healthy.

DEAD Removing all dead wood minimizes entry points for pests and diseases.

DISEASED Eliminate diseased parts, cutting back to a healthy branch or bud.

DAMAGED Remove broken or injured branches as close to the parent limb as possible.

When to Hire, When to DIY

Pruning a large or even a modest-size tree is a big—and potentially hazardous—job that is best left to a pro.

Hire a certified arborist when you feel the least bit uncomfortable about doing the job yourself. Leave it to a certified arborist to cut large, heavy branches, work near power lines, and prune high into a tree. An arborist is trained to work safely with a chainsaw and other equipment, even near houses, fences, and other structures.

Arborists can also evaluate trees for problems caused by insects, diseases, and nutritional imbalances and provide solutions. Problems caught early are easier and less costly to resolve. When contacting a reputable arborist, ask for references, proof of insurance, professional credentials, and a written estimate.

The right way to prune

Pruning is not complicated, once you understand a few basic principles to ensure success. These guidelines hold true whether you prune trees or shrubs.

Choose the right tool Always use clean, sharp tools. To avoid damage to the plant and the tool, select the right-size tool for the branch you will prune. Use a pruning saw on branches larger than 1 to 1½ inches in diameter. Pruners work best on small branches. Use loppers on branches an inch or so in diameter.

left top Let a certified arborist with the skills and equipment handle large, high, and precarious pruning jobs. **left bottom** Professional arborists clean up after themselves, removing all the debris after trimming your tree.

Choose the right time There isn't a single best time for pruning. Late winter is an ideal time for pruning many trees and shrubs because they are dormant then and it is easier to see what needs to be pruned. Late-winter pruning promotes fast regrowth in spring. There are exceptions.

Oaks and crabapples should be pruned in winter while dormant to keep diseases and insects from invading. Some trees— such as maples, birches, and magnolias— bleed sap heavily when pruned in late winter, which causes little harm but can be avoided by pruning after the trees are fully leafed out in late spring or early summer.

Summer is the best time to remove dead branches when they stand out. Prune spring-flowering trees and shrubs right after they finish flowering in spring. Trees and shrubs that bloom during summer and into fall are best pruned in late winter or early spring as soon as annual growth begins. Refrain from fall pruning because it stimulates new growth that could be killed by winter cold.

Prune anytime Suckers; water sprouts; branches that are dead, diseased, or damaged.

Make the right cuts Holding the cutting blade closest to the trunk or main stem, make a clean cut without tearing the bark. Avoid leaving a stub, which is unsightly and provides entry for pests and diseases. Cut just outside the branch collar or the swelling where the branch begins.

LOW-MAINTENANCE GARDENING TIP

FIX A STORM-DAMAGED TREE

Depend on a certified arborist to evaluate a tree for its species, location, and contribution to the landscape, as well as to estimate the cost to prune, repair, or replace.

Right Tool Use short- or long-handled shears to cut small branches. Switch to a pruning saw for larger branches.

Right Time Pruning in late winter allows you to see the shape of a dormant (not growing) plant.

Right Cut Prune with the blade nearest the branch collar (the swelling where branch meets trunk).

Disinfect Shears Clean shears between pruning jobs. Rub the blades with a disinfectant to prevent the spread of disease.

Pruning Trees

Removing dead or problematic branches is necessary at different times in a tree's life.

Pruning young trees encourages strong natural forms and leads to less work later. There's no need to prune a newly planted tree unless it has damaged or dead branches. Give it a year to establish before pruning. Over the next few years, prune annually to remove poorly positioned branches (crossing or competing) and encourage the tree to develop ideal form.

Established trees need occasional pruning to remove dead branches. If the tree has been neglected, it may be necessary to control size, reduce excess shade, or prevent branches from rubbing against each other, wires, buildings, or vehicles.

As a rule, cut no more than one-fourth of a tree's branches in one year. If a tree needs extensive renovation, spread the task over two or more years. Cutting more than 25 percent of any tree's branches can compromise its viability.

Cutting large branches

Remove a branch too large to hold in one hand with three separate cuts using a bow saw. Make the correct cuts using the three-step process instead of trying to do it in one cut, which can rip the bark from the tree. Also avoid leaving a stub, which will decay eventually and become a harbor for pests.

The first cut should be made on the underside of the branch within 6 inches of the trunk. The second cut should be made on the top of the branch 2 to 3 inches from the initial cut. Make the third cut just outside the branch collar to remove the stub. Leave the branch collar; it contains chemicals that speed the formation of a callus, healing the wound.

Let pruning wounds heal on their own. Applying tarlike wound dressings is no longer recommended. The treatment does not benefit the tree or speed healing in most cases. Although it may a take a number of years, some trees that have been pruned incorrectly can be improved. When you start to correct a poorly pruned tree, begin by looking for hidden decay in branch stubs. Prune stubs back to healthy wood.

TRIMMING BRANCHES

Shaping and removing dead wood are the two major tree pruning functions, but there are other times that careful cuts make for a healthier tree.

PRUNED YOUNG TREE
It's easier to prune a tree when it is young. Removing a lower branch allows freer movement, such as mowing beneath it.

COMPETITIVE BRANCHES
Sometimes parallel or sharply angled to a main branch, competing branches weaken a maturing tree.

CROSSING BRANCHES
Limbs that cross or rub may lead to decay or death. Leave the branch that best fits the overall structure.

WATER SPROUTS
These soft, fast-growing branches often rise from the trunk or large limbs, taxing the tree's strength.

SUCKERS
Shoots from the trunk base or roots compromise the tree's natural shape and drain its energy.

CUTTING LARGE BRANCHES

Big branches are best removed in steps to avoid damage to the tree—or to you.

1 INITIAL CUT
Saw from the bottom and cut halfway through the branch.

2 TOP CUT
Just beyond the undercut, saw into the top of the branch. Eventually the branch will break at the first cut.

3 FINAL CUT
Just outside the branch collar, saw from the top and let the branch fall.

LOW-MAINTENANCE GARDENING TIP

PRUNE TREES ON A SCHEDULE

After the first or second year in the garden, prune most trees and shrubs annually; prune slow-growing evergreens once every two years. Even small plants and dwarf trees need regular trimming to stay small and tidy.

right Cut just outside the branch collar or swelling near the trunk to speed healing. Do not cut flush with the trunk.

Pruning Evergreens

Needled and broadleaf evergreens require minimal pruning and specific techniques.

Most evergreens need pruning only to remove dead, damaged, or diseased limbs and to preserve the plant's natural form while limiting size.

Needled evergreens

The pruning schedule is less rigid than for other trees and shrubs. Ideally, prune needled evergreens in winter when plants are resting or in late spring or early summer after new growth stops. Go ahead, prune your plants and use the trimmings for holiday decorating.

Pines, spruces, and others that have three or more branches at each node (the spot where buds develop and form new foliage or stems) grow new branches from the tips of each branch. Prune only new growth, called a candle. Arborvitae, juniper, yew, and others grow from random buds and can be pruned or sheared anywhere along the stems.

PRUNE TO REJUVENATE

Cut one-fourth of a shrub's older stems to the ground each year (over four years) in early spring to encourage new growth and side shoot development.

left **Pinching is an** easy method to prune young pine tips. It involves only a thumb and forefinger to ensure more dense growth.

PRUNING BROADLEAF EVERGREENS

Flowering broadleaf evergreens, such as azalea, pyracantha, and camellia, are best pruned right after blooms fade. Prune broadleaf evergreen shrubs without flowers (boxwood) and with berries (holly) in late winter or early spring.

Boxwood Shearing mutilates foliage. Instead, use pruners to snip stems.

Rhododendron Remove faded flowers by snipping or gently snapping off the spent blooms.

HOW TO PRUNE NEEDLED EVERGREENS

The type of plant dictates the pruning technique and the right tool for the job.

SPRUCE Prune select branches to gently shape the evergreen and to allow balanced exposure to sunlight.

YEW Shearing creates a formal shape. It also prompts dense, more vigorous growth.

JUNIPER Selectively prune branches to maintain the evergreen's natural shape while opening it to more light.

Pruning Shrubs

Begin pruning a shrub when it is young for a healthier, better-looking plant as it matures. Established shrubs may need annual pruning to control size and maintain vigor.

Many shrubs grow rapidly, becoming overgrown and excessively twiggy with leafy top growth and bare bottom branches. This top-heavy bushiness eventually obscures the shrub's structure, reduces flowering, and invites fungal disease.

As with trees, annual moderate pruning to maintain a good framework of well-spaced branches works better than severe pruning to rescue plants after years of neglect. Control the size and shape of shrubs by selectively pruning up to one-third of the plant, heading or cutting back individual shoots with pruners. Large woody branches should be cut back to a side branch using loppers and leaving no stub. Prune the shrub to its natural growth habit and shape, from upright to rounded.

Each year remove some top growth or entire branches to allow more light into the plant, resulting in dense, spreading growth at the bottom.

LOW-MAINTENANCE GARDENING TIP

PRUNE BACK THE DEAD

Some shrubs, such as buddleia, are marginally hardy in cold climates. Roots survive harsh winters, but branches do not. Cut the wood close to the ground using loppers in early spring. New growth will follow.

top Remove suckers (vigorous upright growth from roots) to redirect the plant's energy. **middle** Repeat-blooming *Hydrangea macrophylla* varieties bloom on last year's growth. Wait until they leaf out in early spring to prune out deadwood. **bottom** Snipping off spent flowers (called deadheading) of lilac and other bloomers as soon as they fade is another form of pruning.

PRUNING SPRING-FLOWERING SHRUBS

Bloom times of flowering shrubs determines when to trim them.

Spring bloomers flower on branches that grew the previous year, so winter pruning removes limbs that would produce flowers. Prune spring bloomers right after they finish flowering. Pruning encourages new growth on which more buds can grow for best flowering next year.

Late Winter Leaf and flower buds are ready to go.

Early Spring Blooms usually appear first, followed by leaves.

Late Spring Prune these shrubs as soon as flowers fade.

Summer Next year's flower buds develop on new stems.

PRUNING SUMMER-FLOWERING SHRUBS

For best results, prune in late winter into early spring.

Pruning in fall or midwinter leaves open wounds that lose moisture. Pruning cuts made during these times commonly cause dieback, resulting in more pruning in spring to remove stubs. Pruning cuts made just before or during active growth heal quickly and allow time for new growth for summer blooms.

Late Winter By spring, leaf buds, not flower buds, have formed.

Early Spring Prune the shrub before it begins growing.

Late Spring Each cut results in at least two new branches.

Summer New branches produce a wealth of blooms.

Pruning Roses

Begin each growing season by pruning to enhance the health and flowering of roses. Seize the opportunity to encourage vigorous, well-shaped plants.

It's easy to see quick results from pruning roses—more so than with many shrubs. Here are the basic necessities: In early spring, prune dead, damaged, and diseased canes from established plants. Cut back to healthy, green wood. Also cut out crossing canes, weak suckers sprouting from roots, and canes growing into the center of the plant. Open the plant's center to improve air circulation and let in more light, preventing disease.

Snipping off spent flowers throughout the growing season prompts more blooms. Let the last roses of summer wither on the canes to allow plants to prepare for winter by developing hips. Various types of roses have specific pruning needs.

Modern roses, such as floribundas, grandifloras, hybrid teas, and miniatures, bloom on new wood and benefit from removing one-half to two-thirds of plant height and all but three to five canes.

Because climbers bloom on old wood, wait until after flowers fade to cut back some canes older than two years. Prune for a balance of old and new canes to ensure a good display.

Shrub and old garden roses need only light pruning to remove old weak stems and shape plants.

MAKE A CLEAN CUT

Use sharp, clean bypass pruners to cut most canes. Cut thick canes with loppers or a pruning saw. After pruning, clean blades with a weak bleach solution or comparable disinfectant to minimize spreading disease.

ROSE PRUNING TIPS

In late winter or early spring, when a rose resumes growing, green stems, buds, and foliage will indicate where pruning should occur.

Angle Cuts Make all cuts at a 45-degree angle outward (away from the plant's center).

Weak Growth Remove canes thinner than the diameter of a pencil.

Frost Damage Cut back frost-damaged or winter-killed canes (brown or black) to healthy green wood.

Remove Suckers Cut off weak suckers growing from roots.

Clean Up Remove debris from around the bush that can spread disease.

left Snipping roses, whether fresh or spent, is a form of pruning that benefits the plant. **above top** Prune like a pro, cutting ¼ inch above a bud or five-leaflet leaf at a 45-degree angle. **above bottom** The fruits of roses, rose hips, develop at the end of the flowering season.

Common or meadow violets bloom in spring that can become troublesome in lawns and gardens, reproducing by seeds and by creeping roots and rhizomes. Pick the flowers or pull the plants to minimize them.

LOW-MAINTENANCE GARDENING TIP

DISTINGUISH WEEDS FROM FLOWERS

Learn to recognize weeds common in your region, distinguishing between their appearance as seedlings and mature plants. If you're stumped in identifying a weed, send a sample or photo to your extension service. Sometimes weeds are a matter of opinion: One gardener's wildflowers (sweet violets, dandelions, oxalis) are the bane of a neighbor's weed-free lawn.

Weeding: The Basics

Don't let weeds rob your garden or lawn of health and beauty. These interlopers compete with flowers for water and nutrients.

It's often said that weeds are uninvited plants growing in the wrong place. Although weed seeds lurk in almost any soil, most weeds don't become a problem because they never get the light needed to germinate. But when you cultivate soil, weed seeds inevitably surface and sprout among desirable plants.

Weeds compromise the health and welfare of edible and ornamental plants as well as turfgrasses, competing for nutrients and moisture. Weeds harbor disease pathogens as well as insects and their eggs. Left unchecked, weeds can take over.

Understanding pests

It helps to know the difference between annual and perennial weeds, and to understand how they grow, to determine the best approach to weed control. Most weeds are shallow-rooted annuals that complete their life cycle in one growing season but produce masses (even thousands) of seeds. They germinate in spring or fall and can be prevented. Annuals include crabgrass, foxtail, and ragweed.

Perennial weeds, such as dandelion and creeping charlie, grow tenaciously in ever-expanding patches. Spreading by seeds or roots, they live for years once established.

Remove weeds before they bloom and set seeds for another crop or remove the entire root system.

SHADE OUT WEEDS

Some vegetable crops take care of weeding chores by shading the soil enough to prevent weed seeds from germinating and by crowding them out. Notice how weeds are suppressed by the dense canopy of these crops: bean, corn, cucumber, melon, pumpkin, and squash.

Fibrous Roots
Soil-clinging roots of foxtail and purslane can be pulled easily en masse.

Seedheads
Pull weeds such as plantain before they develop seeds and grow into obnoxious hordes.

Taproot
Carefully dig weeds with long, deep, or assertive roots, such as wild grapevine, to eliminate them.

Common Weeds

Although weed species number in the hundreds, a relative handful are responsible for most problems.

If you could control most common weeds, it would be by doing these three things: Prevent them. Use mulch. Avoid allowing weeds to develop seedheads.

A single mature weed can produce tens of thousands of seeds in one season. Get familiar with various weed life cycles to control them in your garden. Eliminate small patches of a weed before it gains a foothold.

Practice the weed-control methods shown on the pages ahead. Otherwise, keep expectations realistic: There is no such thing as perfect weed control.

Weeds can grow anywhere, and they do—in lawns, gardens, cracks in sidewalks, gutters, and wherever roots can survive. The most noxious weeds, such as kudzu, poison ivy, and Japanese knotweed, grow up into trees, only to make eradication more difficult.

Bindweed This perennial climber has small white trumpet flowers. It twines tightly around garden plants.

Crabgrass Spreading easily by growing roots where stems touch soil, this annual lawn bully requires careful pulling.

Dandelion Lobed leaves and yellow flowers grow from the perennial's long taproot. The flowers turn to puffy seedheads.

Foxtail Dense, fuzzy seedheads appear on this 2- to 3-foot-tall annual at summer's end.

Creeping Charlie The creeping stems of perennial ground ivy root where they touch soil, spreading across lawns and into gardens. Dig the roots.

Purslane This drought-tolerant annual thrives in poor, compacted soil. Pull the taproot carefully.

Oxalis With cloverlike leaves and tiny yellow flowers, this perennial grows a taproot in sun or shade.

Plantain The wide leaves of this perennial smother turf. Its presence signals compacted soil.

Lamb's-quarters Yank the annual plants, taproot and all, before they mature at 3 to 4 feet and cast thousands of seeds.

Ragweed, common This 2- to 4-foot-tall annual with ferny foliage grows from a taproot and tortures allergy sufferers.

Spurge, prostrate Seeds of this ground-hugging annual sprout all summer. Pull the entire taproot.

Thistle Known for its prickly leaves, this fast-spreading perennial has underground stems that colonize.

Dandelions and some other weeds are difficult to pull because they have long taproots. If you don't remove every bit of the root, the weed will soon grow back.

Controlling Weeds

This unending task begins as soon as the ground thaws or plants begin growing in the spring.

If you are diligent in weeding throughout spring, summer weeding chores may not be overwhelming. As summer progresses, more varieties of weed species crop up, prompted by warmer soil. Opportunities continue for you to uproot weeds and their seedlings and banish seedheads.

Control tactics

Many gardeners think of weed pulling as a meditative or therapeutic task: simple, repetitive, productive. For best results, remove weeds as soon as they appear, while roots are undeveloped. Pull weeds after rain or irrigation, when soil is damp. Gather and trash weeds to prevent seeds and roots from sprouting.

Turn to a few trusty tools designed to make weeding easy. Some tools are specialized; others are multipurpose. Your choice will depend on how a weed grows and how you like to remove them. Use mulch as a tool, too: Spread 2 to 3 inches of mulch on open ground, especially after weeding, to prevent new weeds from starting.

Herbicides or chemical weed killers act on some weeds. Preemergent herbicides prevent annual weeds but interfere with all seed germination. Applying them in fall is best. Post-emergent herbicides act on plants that already have leaves.

Less-toxic solutions

Resourceful gardeners practice several weed control methods.

Scalding them Pour boiling water carefully from a teakettle onto tenacious weeds.

Eating them Many weeds are otherwise known as wild edible plants. Dandelion, purslane, lamb's-quarters, and others have long been foraged for spring salads. Some weeds (nightshades) are toxic—beware.

WEEDS REVEAL HEALTHY SOIL NEEDS

Some weeds (purslane, plantain) indicate compacted soil and a need for aeration. Excessive weeds may indicate that the soil is high—maybe too high—in nitrogen.

WEED-CONTROL METHODS

With so many different weeds sprouting in lawns and gardens, there isn't one simple solution—there are many. To keep on top of weeds, various control methods are usually necessary on a regular basis throughout the growing season. Discover which methods and tools work best for you.

1. DIG AND PULL A hand-weeding tool loosens soil and roots at once with a little leverage.

2. WITHOUT A TRACE It isn't easy to get all the roots of creeping charlie, but a cultivator helps get the job done.

3. DON'T TOUCH A warren hoe does the dirty work of uprooting a painfully prickly thistle.

4. ORGANIC OPTION Corn gluten meal is an organic preemergent herbicide that controls some grassy and broadleaf weeds.

5. MANUAL LABOR Rainy weather brings on lush weed growth. Pulling weeds is easiest after rain.

6. DIGGING DEEP A well-designed hand weeder reaches deep to pop out the whole taproot of a weed such as purslane.

Pest Control: The Basics

Knowing that something is amiss and knowing what to do about it are very different. Begin by observing and learning to identify pests.

Pests, including insects, animals, weeds, and diseases, are inevitable in a garden. Their presence is an opportunity to test your mettle without turning your yard into a war zone. Savvy gardeners learn how to work with nature to promote healthy plants with healthy soil and to manage the garden ecosystem through observation, identification, and prevention.

A daily walk in the garden, with a careful look at leaves, stems, flowers, and the ground around plants, helps to spot signs of a problem in time to try effective controls. With practice, you'll learn how to recognize a problem and identify its cause.

Pest detective

Garden pests and environmental challenges cause a staggering range of symptoms: discoloring, wilting, stunting, curling, and deformation, to name a few. Use the general categories of poor plant growth, damaged foliage, damaged fruit, no fruit, and plant death to begin defining your plant problem and finding a solution.

Many plant problems cause only cosmetic damage; little or no control is necessary for plants to be productive. Although some insects can cause major damage to plants, an amazing number of them are beneficial because they eat undesirable bugs. Too often, people reach for a can of spray at the first sign of any critter.

left top If the affected part of a plant is limited, snip it off and trash it. Identify the problem and possible solutions. **left middle** Look for the pest or identify it by the damage done. Decide whether intervention is required. **left bottom** Early spring is prime time to wipe out weed seedlings before they grow deep roots.

IDENTIFYING INSECTS AND DISEASES

The most common garden problems fall into two categories: insects and diseases. If it's not one of these, the problem may be related to weather, soil condition, or other common situations. A weak or stressed plant is more susceptible to pests. Look for answers on the Internet, a local gardening hotline, or university extension office.

Chewing Insects
Damage from caterpillars and other insects includes holes and chewed marks in leaves.

Sucking Insects
Damage from spider mites and other insects comes from them sucking plant sap and spreading diseases.

Marred Leaves Leaf miners are immature stages of flies, wasps, beetles, or moths. The larvae make winding or blotchy mines on foliage.

Disease Symptoms
Viruses, fungi, and bacteria are responsible for a range of plant problems, from spotted foliage to wilting.

Lawn Problems Brown or dead patches of lawn may be due to disease, insects, dog urine, weather, or chemical spill.

Environmental Factors Blossom end rot is caused by inadequate calcium. Dry conditions or excessive nitrogen can make calcium in soil unavailable to plants.

LOW-MAINTENANCE GARDENING TIP

KEEP COMPOST DISEASE-FREE

When you discover diseased foliage in the garden, remove it right away, but don't add the leaves to the compost pile. Remove the disease-affected foliage from your property to keep other areas from becoming infected.

Preventing Problems

The adage "an ounce of prevention is worth a pound of cure" certainly rings true in the garden.

More often than not, it is much easier to prevent a pest, weed, or disease from infiltrating your garden and causing a problem than it is to eliminate the problem and its cause. In nature, a balance of natural predators and a healthy environment keeps most pests, weeds, and diseases under control. One of a gardener's most essential tasks in gardening is to manage problems with a preventive approach. When problems occur—and they do—a knowing gardener helps the garden to help itself and turns to Earth-friendly solutions when necessary.

Simple strategy

You won't make your garden 100 percent free of pests or weeds, but you can take steps to make it a less inviting target. Many problems are avoided simply by using good gardening practices, promoting healthy soil and plants, and keeping the garden clean. A weak or stressed plant is more susceptible to pests.

Keeping a close eye on the garden enables you to spot problems in the making. A problem caught early is easier to resolve, whether the early stages of a disease, weed seedlings, or a bit of rabbit damage.

Preventive practices become a way of life when gardening. Watering in the morning gives plants a chance to dry during the day, minimizing a damp haven for disease. Spacing plants with plenty of growing room also allows for air circulation. Overcrowding can cause weak plant growth and less air movement, resulting in more problems with insect pests and diseases. Rotating crops minimizes pests and diseases.

Avoid injury to plants. Broken or dead limbs, cuts, bruises, cracks, and insect damage are common sites for infection by disease organisms. Remove and dispose of damaged or dead plant parts.

left Remove spent flowers, dead leaves, fallen fruit, and other debris that can harbor pests and diseases.

PRACTICING PREVENTION

The best thing you can do to prevent pests and diseases is to grow diverse, healthy plants that can resist challenges. Provide the sun exposure, soil conditions, moisture levels, and nutrients that plants need.

Healthy Plants
Purchase the healthiest plants you can find if you don't grow them from seeds.

Healthy Soil Have your soil tested and amend it accordingly. Healthy soil can prevent most insect and disease issues.

Resistant Varieties
Choose disease- and pest-resistant plant varieties. For example, plant only tomato varieties bred to resist wilt diseases.

Fewer Weeds Keep weeds out of beds. Removing them when they're young is easier than wrestling with deep roots or when they've gone to seed.

Problem Plants If a plant shows more stress, diseases, or other problems than most, get rid of it. Roses and other plants harbor disease and pests.

Plant Diversity
Attract beneficial insects with a mix of flowers, vegetables, herbs, fruit trees, shrubs, and vines. Plant diverse and dissimilar species.

AVOID SPREADING DISEASE

LOW-MAINTENANCE GARDENING TIP

When plants are wet with rain or dew, diseases can spread easily. Avoid working in the garden until plants dry out. Adequate spacing of plants and careful watering (of soil, not foliage) also help prevent disease problems.

Beneficial Creatures

In this bug-eat-bug world, your garden will get by with a little help from some insect friends and wildlife allies.

When dealing with insect pests, it is more efficient, economical, and Earth-friendly to support the web of life shared by humans, plants, insects, and other creatures. You don't have to take on pests by yourself. Enlist allies.

How to welcome beneficials

If you encourage beneficial insects and others (birds, bats, toads) to visit and stay in your yard by providing food, water, and shelter, nature will take its course. Most adult beneficial insects need nectar, pollen, or plant sap that is available in a diverse flower garden.

Similarly, insect-eating birds, bats, and toads are attracted to habitats with a wide range of plant types, including sources of food and shelter as well as water. Providing simple housing for birds and bats encourages them to stick around.

Observe the garden regularly and get to know its residents. Of the 1.3 million identified insect species, less than 1 percent are pests. The rest are beneficial. Beneficial insects (green lacewing, ladybird beetle, and praying mantis) prey and feed on pest insects. Beneficial nematodes and other good parasites lay eggs on or in a host to feed on it. They do not harm humans or pets. Likewise, most wasps and bees provide benefits.

Learn to identify beneficial insects of your region and watch how they behave. The delicate green lacewings that are attracted to outdoor lights at night are one of the best suppressors of aphids and other soft-bodied insects by day. If you're concerned that your yard lacks a balanced insect population, you can purchase and release helpful insects in your yard; they may or may not stay.

WELCOME WILDLIFE

Providing food and water sources in your yard encourages birds to visit, feast, drink, and bathe. Trees, shrubs, and vines also provide shelter and nesting places.

opposite, above Ladybugs (aka ladybird beetle) is an aphid-eating insect that may be red or orange. **opposite, far left** Praying mantis is a highly effective insect predator; the mantis preys with strong, quick forelegs. **opposite, middle** Harmless to humans, the yellow-and-black garden spider is an important garden insect predator. **opposite, right** Honeybees and wasps, the irreplaceable pollinators, are among the garden's most important workers. **right** Enlist the aid of birds in pest control. Add to your garden fruitful plants (serviceberry, crabapple, viburnum) and a source of water that will attract birds.

Minimizing Insect Pests

Some pest problems are mainly cosmetic; others can kill plants. Coordinated pest management uses gardening methods of damage control.

Not so long ago, chemicals were the standard approach to controlling garden pests. Today's world of environmental awareness and health consciousness spurs gardeners to avoid using chemicals and to seek alternatives.

Determining your best management strategy entails decisions: Is the problem unsightly or serious? Is it worth the time, effort, or expense to take action? Consider alternative controls and evaluate consequences before you act. Combine control tactics to develop a strategy to maintain a healthy garden.

Physical controls

The least toxic ways to deal with insect pests are simple: Pick troublesome insects or eggs off plants and squish them. If you spot Japanese beetles feasting on your roses, knock them off into a bucket of soap-sudsy water to their demise.

You won't eliminate pests from your garden, but you can control their numbers with a variety of traps and hinder their access to plants with such physical barriers as row covers.

Biological controls

Encourage or even add natural predators and pathogens such as ladybird beetles against scale insects, parasitic nematodes against cucumber beetles, or the bacteria Bt (*Bacillus thuringiensis*) against caterpillars. Biological controls target specific pests and won't wipe out other insects.

Chemical controls

Newer botanical chemicals developed from plants provide effective pest controls with fewer harmful side effects to the environment. If you use a petroleum-based chemical pesticide as a last defense, you will kill beneficial insects along with pests. Read product descriptions and labels carefully. Products made for use on ornamental plants may not be safe for use on edibles.

Keep in mind that most steps taken to manage pests of all kinds require repetition. Insects, weeds, and diseases have life cycles: Repeating a method of pest control several times within a month helps minimize the problem and successive generations.

Insecticidal Soap
A variety of insecticidal soaps, including organic options, are available from garden suppliers to spray on pests.

Physical Barriers
A cloche made from a tomato cage and window screen lets in light and moisture but keeps insect pests away from a tender plant.

LOW-MAINTENANCE GARDENING TIP

MIX UP HOMEMADE INSECTICIDE

A simple mix of 3 to 5 tablespoons liquid soap (castile or Ivory Snow, not detergent) in a gallon of water makes an effective insecticidal soap. Spraying it on soft-bodied insects (aphids, spider mites, whiteflies) coats and kills them on contact.

THE SAFEST SPRAY: WATER

Start with the least-toxic control. Nudge the system, instead of hammering it, to reestablish a healthy balance.

If you feel compelled to spray something on plants infested with aphids or a similar pest, reach for the garden hose. Attach to your garden hose a nozzle that will spray water in a forceful jet. Use a blast of water to chase off aphids and other soft-bodied insects. The force of the water, as well as the water itself, will work quickly to knock off the fragile insects. Do this early in the day, allowing the sun and wind to dry plants afterward.

MAKE STICKY TRAPS

Traps let you know where certain pests are active and when it's time to start putting controls to work.

Traps lure pesky insects onto a sticky surface using an attractive color or insect sex pheromones. A variety of insect pests are attracted to yellow, including whiteflies, aphids, cucumber beetles, flea beetles, fruit flies, fungus gnats, and leaf miners.

It's easy to make yellow sticky traps for use among garden plants or houseplants. This is a nontoxic way to snag pests as they stick to the surface of the card.

Achieve the same effect using a yellow plastic drinking cup, coating the inside with Tanglefoot, and turning the cup upside down over the end of a garden stake. Stand a few stakes with sticky traps among garden plants. Gently shake nearby plants from time to time to dislodge insects, encouraging them to fly off and into the traps.

YELLOW CARD Cut yellow cardstock into 6×8-inch pieces. Attach each card to a stake or hook.

MAKE IT STICKY Brush petroleum jelly or Tanglefoot (from a hardware store or garden center) on both sides of each card.

Problem Insects

You don't want to see your garden ravaged by hungry insects.

The first sign of an insect pest rarely means that a devastating infestation is about to settle on your garden. Most gardens have a small amount of insect damage, and it does not affect the garden's overall appearance. Get out your magnifying glass and have a field day: Learn to identify common insect pests and the damage they cause.

Unwanted insects

Keeping plants as healthy as possible is the first line of defense against insect pests. The next step is learning what the culprits look like and how to control them. Decide how much damage to a plant you can tolerate and then act. In the process, don't let pesky insects get you down.

Aphids They suck plant juices, causing shriveled leaves and wilted flowers. Control: Spray with water or soapy water; release ladybird beetles.

Cabbageworms/ Moths Tan or white moths lay eggs that hatch into leaf-munching caterpillars. Control: Bt (*Bacillus thuringiensis*).

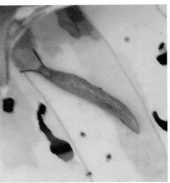

Slugs and Snails Thriving in damp areas, they rasp holes in leaves and flowers. Control: minimal mulch, traps, bait, diatomaceous earth.

Rose Slugs The larval stage of sawfly wasps chews holes in leaves, leaving veins. Control: Pick off leaves, apply insecticidal soap.

Cucumber Beetles
Striped or spotted, they feed on crops and spread wilt disease. Control: carefully timed release of parasitic nematodes, floating row cover.

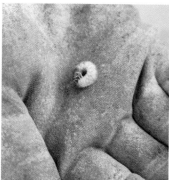

Grubs The larval forms of Japanese and June beetles burrow under lawns. Control: parasitic nematodes.

Japanese Beetles
Look for green and coppery wings. They devour edibles and ornamentals. Control: handpicking, horticultural oil.

Flea Beetles The tiny hopping insects cause shot-hole damage in leaves. Control: horticultural oil, pyrethrum.

Scale Insects Types of these sap feeders may be cottony, soft and waxy, or hard and shellaclike. Control: horticultural oil, dormant oil.

Spider Mites Minuscule arachnids (not insects) sap plants, leaving stippled foliage and tiny webs. Control: Spray with water, citrus oil, or insecticidal soap.

Squash Bugs The sap suckers injure squash, pumpkins, and cucumbers. Control: garden hygiene, crop rotation, handpicking, traps.

Whiteflies The tiny sap suckers raise havoc indoors and outdoors. Control: sticky traps, horticultural oil.

Common Animal Pests

Once you extend a welcome to the wildlife in your area, you may find some animals less desirable than others.

Watching backyard wildlife can be enjoyable, but some animals quickly wear out their welcome when they treat your garden as an all-you-can-eat buffet. Deer have no regard for the hours of loving care you lavish on the roses or the fortune you spend on tulips; for them, the plants are just another meal.

Wild animals known to coexist with people and pets can damage gardens and homes, carry diseases, or pose a health threat to pets or family members. When the damage is serious enough to warrant intervention, it's important to identify the cause of the problem and determine your coping strategy. A rabbit can devour seedlings or sprouting lilies overnight, chomping off stems near ground level. Deer can decimate just about any plants, yanking roots right out of the ground and leaving their uneven bite marks on shrubs and flowering plants. Woodchucks and gophers inflict damage lower to the ground, nipping stems neatly with their sharp teeth.

Can you tell the difference among the tunnels of different rodents? Gophers leave a fan-shape pile of earth around half an entry hole. Moles excavate a perfect circle of soil around the hole. Voles tunnel close to the soil's surface without leaving mounds of earth. If one of these rodents is tunneling in your yard, it is also feasting on your garden.

Find a humane way to discourage an animal pest or trap it for relocation. For assistance, call your local animal control office, a local wildlife sanctuary, or a professional pest control specialist.

LOW-MAINTENANCE GARDENING TIP

FOILING DEER

Hungry deer will eat almost any plant. But they tend to avoid plants with toxic foliage (daffodils, foxglove, rhubarb), fuzzy foliage (lamb's-ears, black-eyed susan), prickles (yucca, barberry, pine), and fragrant foliage (artemisia, lavender, catmint).

left During breeding season, bucks aggressively rub their antlers against trees. Deer severely damaged these aspen trees.

GARDEN VISITORS

Your lovely garden will look beautiful to creatures great and small. And some may also find your flowers and foliage delectable.

TRAP AND RELEASE

You can catch small critters, such as moles and gophers, in baited traps, then relocate them—but check local regulations before turning to this method. First try to repel, exclude, or otherwise deter the rascals before resorting to trapping and releasing them elsewhere.

Deer A widespread pest, deer damage all kinds of plants. Tall fences slow the agile jumpers.

Rabbit This rodent favors tender shoots and young plants. It gnaws bark, twigs, and buds in winter.

Raccoon Foraging at night on compost, fruits, and vegetables, raccoons can be deterred by a dog or an electric fence.

Squirrel This pest raids birdfeeders, eats bulbs, and nests in attics and garages. Trim tree branches away from rooflines.

Woodchuck A strong rodent (or groundhog) digs big holes. It eats shoots, flower buds, and fruit.

Rabbits devour garden plants, especially tender young growth in spring. Fencing deters them.

Deterring Animal Pests

Instead of taking action after the damage is done, protect your garden from hungry critters.

You have plenty of options when taking a preventive approach to animal pests. Some methods are more effective than others. A combination of a barrier and a repellent often produces better results because the methods by themselves have limitations. Repellents must be reapplied after a rain. Fencing select areas or plants may be possible, but enclosing an entire yard may not.

Some gardeners have dogs to keep deer and other wild creatures at bay. Put your faithful friend to work in your yard, especially after dusk and in the spring when deer and others are most active.

There are also ways to make your property less hospitable to deer. Plant the most-vulnerable plants closest to the house, protected by fencing. Avoid planting fruit trees and susceptible ornamental plants such as roses along your yard's periphery. Deer dwell at edges of woods, graze their way into the open from the periphery, and retreat to the woods for safety.

Deer fencing—at least 8 feet tall or electric—works, but it is not always suitable, especially in suburbia. Installing two parallel 5-foot fences about 5 feet apart, and planting shrubs in between them, is effective. It's also a more attractive alternative to an 8-foot barrier.

left top Keep out deer by building a sturdy fence tall enough (at least 8 feet) to keep out these agile creatures. It can be pretty as well as practical. **left bottom** Heavy-duty garden netting shields a cherry crop from hungry birds.

PEST-CONTROL OPTIONS

Discouraging deer, rabbits, raccoons, voles, and other pesky creatures requires gardeners to be proactive and resourceful. Use homemade or commercial deterrents such as these. Alternate repellents throughout the year for maximum effect because deer and others lose their fear of the familiar.

Repellent Spray A smelly or distasteful spray formulated to thwart rabbits, deer, and others works until it must be replenished.

Low Fencing A barrier such as waffle fencing deters rabbits, but 24-inch-tall wire excludes them, especially when buried in 6 inches of soil.

Tree Wrap Wrap a sturdy shield around young trees, from below soil level to above the snow line. Remove it by summer.

Wire Cloche A portable and temporary device covers a tender young plant such as a lily, protecting it from grazing rabbits.

Tall Fencing Stakes and mesh combine to make an economical 8-foot-tall enclosure for a vegetable garden in a neighborhood rife with deer.

Wire Wrap Hardware cloth, cut to form a simple wrap, keeps animals away from a young blueberry plant.

LOW-MAINTENANCE GARDENING TIP

CONTROL MOLES

It is a common misconception that controlling grubs in your lawn will get rid of moles. Although moles do eat grubs, their number one food source is earthworms. Unless the grub population is high (more than 10 per square foot), control isn't needed. Trapping moles is the most effective way to eliminate them from your yard.

Common Diseases

Protect your plants from debilitating diseases. Learn to recognize the symptoms and practice prevention.

Diseases are caused by bacteria, fungi, and viruses. Bacteria are single-celled organisms that live on various kinds of organic matter. Unable to survive in the open, bacteria live inside plants and are transferred plant to plant by insects, water, and hands. Fungi are minute organisms that live on plants and cause visible symptoms. They spread most often via water, wind, and insects. Viruses are the smallest of disease vectors and the most difficult to control. They are typically spread by insects, but some are spread by seeds and tools.

Generally for a disease to occur, organisms must be transported to a susceptible host, such as a stressed plant. Ideal conditions (humid, dry, cloudy) make it possible for the disease to thrive.

Prevention is the best defense against pathogens. Above all, start with disease-resistant plant varieties and practice garden hygiene. A disease-prevention strategy includes these:

Site plants far enough apart to allow air circulation.

Manage susceptible plants, growing them in the recommended amount of sun, keep them well-watered, and don't over- or underfertilize.

Spray healthy leaves of susceptible plants with a homemade fungicide (recipe far right).

Remove and trash affected plant parts.

left top Use a fungicide as a preventive rather than a cure for disease.
left bottom Some plants are susceptible to disease, such as powdery mildew on this phlox. Other vulnerable plants include rose, iris, tomato, lilac, and zinnia.

NOTORIOUS DISEASES

Leaf spots are one of the most common symptoms of disease, whether caused by bacteria, fungi, or viruses. Other symptoms of disease include sudden wilting, ragged or curling leaves, deformed flowers or fruit, and generally discolored or mottled foliage.

Bacterial Spot Most common in damp, humid weather, the disease can be controlled by avoiding working among wet plants.

Black Spot Especially common on roses, the fungal disease causes dark splotches on leaves and leaf drop.

Powdery Mildew A fungus resembling white powder on foliage thrives during dry, humid weather.

Rose Rosette This viral disease spread by a minuscule mite cannot be prevented or cured.

Mosaic Virus Peonies and other plants affected by this or other viruses should be destroyed to prevent spread of the incurable disease.

Rust Spread by several fungus species, rust deforms leaves with orange, gold, or brown-red spots and weakens plants.

LOW-MAINTENANCE GARDENING TIP

MAKE YOUR OWN FUNGICIDE

Spray healthy leaves of particularly susceptible plants with a solution of 1 teaspoon of baking soda and 1 teaspoon of horticultural oil in a quart of water. Adding one of these antifungal ingredients to your spray can boost its effectiveness: 2 crushed cloves of garlic or 2 tablespoons of neem oil (derived from the tropical neem tree).

The Easiest Plants

Start with easy-care plants for a beautiful low-maintenance garden.

Flowers and Foliage: The Basics

Using basic techniques, you can plan and plant a beautiful, healthy garden and enjoy it—trading minimum fuss for maximum satisfaction.

Flowers attract many to gardening, but blooms are fleeting, sometimes lasting only a day. Foliage carries the garden when there are few if any flowers. Gardens that include flowering and foliage plants put on a continually changing show, from emerging sprouts to buds, blooms, and seedheads. The interplay of plant heights, bloom times, and textures is part of a bigger picture.

Proven performers

If trees, shrubs, and vines are the garden's hard-working stage crew, then perennials star while annuals fill the chorus line. Where a complete array of plants works together, rave reviews typically result.

Selected for overlapping bloom times, flowering plants can perform in waves from early spring through summer's hottest days and fall's coolest ones until frost closes the show. Often chosen for longevity, perennials unfurl new foliage and flowers each year, sometimes spreading into impressive colonies. Although annuals last for only one growing season, they're tapped for endurance and sustained color from spring into fall.

Most perennials bloom only for a few weeks. Gardens planted only with perennials may experience lulls in flowering as seasons change, but gardens that include colorful foliage and annuals boast a longer-lasting display.

left Flowering and foliage plants work magic in the garden, transforming an ordinary yard into a charming one.

TRY OUT COMBOS

LOW-MAINTENANCE GARDENING TIP

Use a large container to try plant combinations you'd like to see in your garden, such as annuals and perennials with a small shrub, for a season. If the combo works, transplant it into the garden in early fall and replace the annuals next year.

Garden dreams

Before you buy a plant or dig a hole, determine your goals for a flowering garden. Your rationale may involve problem-solving, such as transforming an area where grass won't grow, disguising an eyesore, or dressing a damp area with pretty plants. You may want to improve a view or attract more hummingbirds to the yard.

Half the fun is dreaming. But having a purpose saves time, money, and effort. Also, think about your personal preferences for the aesthetic attributes of plants. You may like the wild prairie look of massed perennials growing among ornamental grasses or the serene effect of a white-flower, silver-foliage garden.

Grow what appeals to you, realizing that preferences change. Trees grow and create more shade. Plants die and offer opportunities to try new ones.

GET FLOWERS ON A BUDGET

LOW-MAINTENANCE GARDENING TIP

Start some of your plants from easy-to-grow seeds and transplant them into the garden in spring. Purchasing flats that hold multiple cell packs of seedlings (typically 36 or more) is also economical.

FLOWER GARDEN SECRETS

Follow these guidelines to successful flower gardening. Enjoy the process, knowing that even accidents of nature are sometimes gardening's greatest gifts.

Know what you want. Focus on your garden's purpose: Dress up the foundation. Attract butterflies. Grow flowers for cutting.

Start small. Gardening takes time, so be realistic about what you can manage. Work in stages over several years.

Choose tough plants. Select plants with long-season appeal, as well as tolerance to drought, pests, and diseases.

Match plants to place. Work with your site and choose plants adapted to the light, soil, and climate.

Begin with good soil. Abundant flowers grow in healthy soil. Organic material improves most soil.

Easy Annuals

For sheer flower power, annuals excel. Choose them for inexpensive, nearly instant color—you'll learn to love them for so much more.

Annuals live for the moment or at least a season. They are genetically programmed to complete their life cycle—from seed to mature plant to seed again—within one year. By concentrating their energy into intense performance, these fast-growing and free-flowering plants make gardens come alive with color.

Whether you choose annuals for their flowers or foliage, they come in almost any color, form, and size. Whatever your growing conditions, there are annuals just right for your garden.

Annuals are among the most versatile of gardening tools. Use them to fulfill creative gardening goals.

Paint Create bold swaths with mass plantings or make rich patterns with contrasting plants. Growing annuals allows you to change your mind and color scheme every growing season.

Weave Tuck annuals among perennials to extend bloom times, bridge the seasons, refresh displays, and keep color growing strong.

Experiment Find favorites among the newest improved varieties or old-fashioned beauties. Turn to some for sweet scents and others for cutting qualities.

Although some are sensitive to heat or chill, plenty of annuals keep up the growathon from frost to frost. Some annuals (cleome, bachelor's button, larkspur, and others) are such successful self-seeders, they act like perennials and return year after year. Others really are perennials, but their tropical origin and tender nature means they must be grown as annuals in temperate and colder climates.

Annuals are most budget friendly when planted from seeds. Flats or cell packs of seedlings from greenhouses and garden centers are also economical.

left A flat of annual seedlings such as verbena gives you an economical way to add long-lasting color to the garden.

LOW-MAINTENANCE GARDENING TIP

PLANT COOL- AND WARM-SEASON ANNUALS

Cool-season annuals (pansy, stock, twinspur) usually do best in cool soils during fall and spring. Where winters are mild, they can be planted in fall for early spring blooms. Warm-season annuals (marigold, impatiens, angelonia) grow and flower best in warm months when there is no threat of frost.

EASIEST ANNUALS

The choice of annuals is so vast and versatile, you'll find a delightful variety to brighten any spot in your garden. Annuals will grow and bloom for any gardener. With wide range of colors and heights, they allow freedom in garden design and adapt to various planting times.

1. BEGONIA, WAX (*Begonia × semperflorens*) This bedding plant forms 12-inch mounds with nonstop blooms in a range of conditions, from sun to shade.

2. COSMOS (*Cosmos*) These old-fashioned favorites, 18 to 48 inches tall, provide daisylike flowers for fresh arrangements. Sow seeds in warm garden soil.

3. GERANIUM (*Pelargonium × hortorum*) Easy and vigorous, these popular plants bloom abundantly in sun or light shade. Some varieties have showy or fragrant leaves.

4. IMPATIENS (*Impatiens*) The lush, mounded plants, in a range of heights and flower types, brighten shade with continuous color. Choose New Guinea types for sunny spots.

5. MARIGOLD (*Tagetes*) A dazzling array of types and forms grow 6 to 30 inches tall for bedding, edging, cutting, pots, and kitchen gardens. Most marigolds have a pungent scent.

6. PANSY (*Viola*) Chilly weather brings out the best in charming pansies and their viola cousins. Choose from various faces and colors. Plant them in early fall or spring.

7. PETUNIA (*Petunia*) Dependable all-season bloomers, these hybrids offer amazing variations of flower color, pattern, and form on bushy or trailing plants.

8. ZINNIA (*Zinnia*) Grow zinnias for their flowers in an array of bright colors and sizes. They attract butterflies and hummingbirds and make long-lasting bouquets.

9. SAGE, ANNUAL (*Salvia*) Blue sage (*S. farinacea*) and scarlet sage (*S. splendens*) form ribbons of constant color in beds. The plants love sun, heat, and well-drained soil.

10. VINCA (*Catharanthus roseus*) For beds, borders, or baskets, this nonstop bloomer with glossy foliage is undaunted by heat and drought and doesn't need deadheading.

Planting Annuals

When you grow annuals, every planting season is an opportunity for a new look and color scheme in your garden.

Many annuals are so simple to start from seeds that a child can do it. Planting annuals from seeds means you can start the gardening season indoors weeks before trees leaf out. You can line up a few pots on a sunny windowsill or sprout an entire garden from seed. Growing plants from seed saves money and does wonders for self-confidence.

Most plants bloom within 50 to 70 days after planting. Check the "days to maturity" on seed packets, then count backward on your calendar, starting with the last average frost date in your region, to determine the best time for seed sowing. If you live in a frost-free area, plant seeds in late winter or early spring. When seedlings have strong root systems that fill out their packs or pots, they're ready to transplant.

Bedding plants—seedlings—are sold in multicell packs, multipack flats, and larger containers. These days, more gardeners choose to start with popular annuals in 4- or 6-inch pots for instant-garden appeal. Bedding plants are ready for transplanting, like any seedlings, into prepared soil after frost threat has passed. Plant seedlings at the same level as they were growing in their nursery pots.

Water seedlings a day or two before transplanting because cells packs and small pots dry out quickly. If possible, plant on a cool, cloudy day because harsh sun, heat, or wind stresses seedlings. Otherwise, planting late on a sunny day allows the tender plants to acclimate overnight. Always water plants as soon as they're transplanted.

SOWING SEEDS

Sow Directly Calendula and some other annuals can be sown in warm, cultivated garden soil after frost danger has passed.

Protect Seedlings Lay twigs over a seedbed to protect germinating seeds from hungry birds. Once the seedlings have two sets of leaves, remove the twigs.

POTTING UP SEEDLINGS

Seedling to Cell When seedlings have developed at least two sets of mature leaves, pull them gently apart and plant each in its own cell of potting mix.

Cell to Pot When a seedling's root system fills a cell, move it into a pot. Transplant each seedling into a 3- or 4-inch pot and you'll have bigger, stronger (garden-ready) plants within a few weeks.

Planting annuals in a new bed

If your goal is to have masses of color in a hurry with minimal cost, rely on bedding plants for one dazzling summer-long show.

Bedding plants get their name from Victorian gardeners, who filled tidy beds with compact colorful annuals in patterned rows. This still-popular approach to planting transforms a new bed into a carpet of color within weeks. Space plants closer together than recommended for faster effects and farther apart for economy.

A long list of annual all-stars, from ageratum to zinnia, stands up and spreads color under the hottest sun. Most gardeners are limited to growing the varieties that local garden centers offer, but greenhouses often have more varied selections. Every new gardening season brings a crop of new varieties with outstanding vigor, nonstop blooms, and fun new colors that combine easily.

Help bedding plants continue their show by shearing them by one-third their size in mid- to late summer. Fertilize the plants and watch them bloom with renewed vigor.

LOW-MAINTENANCE GARDENING TIP

START FLOWERS FROM SEED

Plants recommended for first-time seed starters include calendula, celosia, cosmos, marigold, pansy, sunflower, and zinnia. Varieties of these annuals can be sown directly in the garden.

BEDDING OUT PLANTS

Create a swath of bold color by massing bright annuals in a bed together. They will spread out quickly and bloom until frost.

1 REMOVE PACKS
Squeeze and release a seedling's root ball from a cell pack or pot. Set each seedling in place, spacing them as directed on the plant tag.

2 PLACE PLANTS
Equal spacing between plants and rows creates a uniform look. Use a trowel to make planting holes slightly larger than plant root balls.

3 PROMPT ROOTING
Pinch off any flowers to prompt rooting. Sacrificing those blooms makes a difference in the new plantings' success.

4 WATER WELL
Water each plant thoroughly after planting, using a transplant or starter solution (dilute plant food) to help plants overcome stress.

above, left Most annuals are ready for transplanting six to eight weeks after they're sown from seeds. Transplants begin rooting and growing in the garden within a couple of weeks.

Easy Perennials

Where there's a garden, there will be work and there will be pleasure. The goal is having a lovely garden where you can do the kind of gardening you enjoy most.

Just because perennials come back each year does not mean they are care-free. But if you aim to keep your garden design simple and avoid prima donna plants, you can have a beautiful garden as well as plenty of time to sit back and enjoy it.

The growing garden

Plants change as they age, and their needs change, too. A garden in infancy is filled with small, cute plants with lots of space between them. It may be hard to visualize a mature 'Sum and Substance' hosta reaching 7 feet across.

In an adolescent garden, plants may be lazy (overly floppy), moody (refusing to bloom), or obstinate (refusing to grow at all). In middle age, plants begin to mature; the garden fills in

and looks spectacular. Eventually plants lose their youthful good looks and no longer bloom well. The time comes for replacement, division, or other changes.

Perennial challenges

Although perennials can be used to advantage in any garden, they present challenges, too. There are countless species of perennials and many plant-specific care techniques. The changing nature of a perennial garden requires ample space for plants to reach their potential. Some perennials can wreak havoc, spreading aggressively. All of these challenges are outweighed by the beauty, longevity, and adaptability of perennials.

Color
Start with a single-color scheme. Add hues to build one color family. Change it up with an accent color or neutral white.

Texture
Plants' touchable surfaces reflect or absorb light, creating textural effects. Leaf and flower shapes and sizes also play into this quality.

Form
Juxtapose plant shapes and sizes to give a garden variety, rhythm, balance, and scale. Repetition creates cohesiveness.

Focal Point
Choose a plant or an object (birdbath, arbor, planter) that draws the eye to rest. It must stand out, while the garden exists in relation to it.

LOW-MAINTENANCE GARDENING TIP

CHOOSE LONG-LIVED PERENNIALS

Start your garden with a few long-lived plants, then find companions that complement, contrast, and flower in other time frames. Be sure to include perennials with striking foliage and small shrubs. Your garden will ultimately be greater than each added part. Combining plants for dramatic effect will become easier as you have more gardening successes.

RELIABLE FLOWERING PERENNIALS

When you plan a perennial garden, it's natural to focus on flowers for creating a colorful display throughout the growing season. Form the backbone of your garden with enduring bloomers such as these. Hardy plants with survivor instincts (tolerating drought, disease, and pests) should also top your plant list for an undemanding garden.

1. CATMINT (*Nepeta*) Tolerating heat, drought, wind, and foot traffic, catmint grows easily in Zones 4–10 and boasts mounds of fragrant foliage and lasting flowers.

2. IRIS (*Iris*) Iris grow from bulbs or rhizomes. They include bearded and beardless groups in the spring-summer bloom season. Many are hardy in Zones 3–8.

3. COREOPSIS (*Coreopsis*) Easy-growing and long-blooming, the plants tolerate heat and drought but flop over in rich, wet soil in Zones 4–10. Deadhead to encourage flowers.

4. CONEFLOWER (*Echinacea*) Tough and fuss-free in Zones 3–10, coneflowers beckon butterflies, bees, and birds with blooms summer through fall.

5. SPIKE SPEEDWELL (*Veronica*) Easy to grow for long-season color from summer until frost, it's a natural choice for cottage or wildlife gardens in Zones 4–10.

6. DAYLILY (*Hemerocallis*) The robust plants can cope with nearly any growing condition, but they're susceptible to hungry deer, rabbits, and slugs. Zones 3–11.

7. PHLOX (*Phlox*) Various species bloom lavishly in nearly every season in Zones 2–9. Plant mildew-resistant varieties of tall garden phlox.

8. PENSTEMON (*Penstemon*) The flowers attract hummingbirds. Plant it in drifts, with crowns planted just above soil level, for a strong flower show in Zones 2–10.

9. SAGE (*Salvia*) Valued for its long bloom season from spring to fall, this tough plant tolerates heat, drought, and humidity in Zones 4–10.

10. YARROW (*Achillea*) This hardy North American native has ferny foliage that deer and rabbits resist eating. It's fast growing and drought tolerant for Zones 2–10.

Planting Perennials

Planting is easy, but attention to detail makes the difference between plants that thrive and those that merely survive. Some plants have special planting needs.

Because perennials grow in the same spot for years, it's essential to prepare the soil. Work in loads of organic amendments and make it well draining.

Start perennials from seeds, bare roots, or plants. Or start from divisions or cuttings gleaned from friends or neighbors. Planting requirements vary for each plant, but a few general parameters apply to all.

The best times to plant are when soil and weather conditions favor strong root growth. Spring and early fall planting give plants time to establish roots before summer or winter arrives.

Dig planting holes twice as wide as the plant root ball. Loosen the sides and bottom of the planting hole to help roots spread. Set the crowns of most plants at soil level. If planted too deep, the plant can rot.

Avoid planting in static rows; instead, place plants in triangles or stagger them for more pleasing results. Leave enough space between plants for root growth, air circulation, and mature growth. Plants set too closely together will compete for water and nutrients, eventually crowd one another, and require transplanting or division.

Special situations

Perennials with taproots (butterfly weed, columbine, cushion spurge, Oriental poppy) that grow straight down from the crown typically resent transplanting. Take extra care to plant them deeply without damaging or disturbing the roots.

Other plants fare best when provided with especially well-draining conditions from the start. Plants such as lavender and spring-flowering bulbs originated in rocky, fast-draining places; they benefit from a gravelly planting place.

Planting can be stressful for any plant, so handle each one with care and avoid cutting or tearing roots.

Nurtured throughout spring in a nursery pot until it reaches garden-ready size, a foxglove transplant can be moved into the garden where it will bloom in summer.

PLANTING A BARE-ROOT PERENNIAL

Dormant perennials sold without soil have bare roots and need to be planted as early as possible in spring. If the bare roots you purchase have become mushy or dried out, ask the vendor for a replacement. If it's too early in the season to dig in the garden, plant bare roots in pots and keep the soil barely moist. This example shows a bleeding heart (perennial) planting.

1 PREPARE TO PLANT

Dig a planting hole and amend the soil. Form a mound at the bottom of the planting hole.

2 PLACE THE BARE ROOT

When set on the mound, the bare root should be at the right depth, with the growing tips or crown at soil level.

3 SATURATE SOIL

Fill in the planting hole and mark the spot with a plant label. Water thoroughly, then apply a layer of mulch.

LOW-MAINTENANCE GARDENING TIP

MOVE PERENNIALS AFTER BLOOMING

If you decide that a plant should be planted in another spot, dig it up and transplant it after it has finished blooming, which is less stressful for the plant. Mark a spot in the garden where you want to relocate it, then transplant at an optimal time: late summer or early spring.

PERENNIAL POINTERS

Start perennials off right in the garden with tips for health and longevity.

MARK THE SPOT

Labeling new plantings helps you remember plant names as well as those that may need extra water.

NURSERY PLANTS

Small, young perennial seedlings benefit from nurserying, or growing in bigger pots for a season.

WELL-DRAINING SOIL

Grit and gravel improve clay soil and make it possible to plant lavender, bulbs, and other plants that need well-draining soil.

IMPROVING DRAINAGE

Poor drainage can kill plants. Add handfuls of drainage-improving mix to a planting hole or more to a larger planting area.

Easy Foliage Plants

Most gardeners are smitten first with flowers, but over time, an appreciation for foliage plants deepens and often grows into a lasting passion. It's no wonder.

Leaves weave tapestries of shapes, textures, and hues in ways that flowers cannot. Colorful flowers grab attention, but they come and go. Foliage creates long-lasting beauty in sun or shade and needs no deadheading—more glory with less work.

Foliage not only creates balance among the bloomers, it also works independently. Foliage-only combinations prove entirely harmonious and satisfying. Even better, foliage is dependable on an ongoing basis, bringing its strengths to the garden from spring through fall.

ALL-STARS FOR SHADE

In the universe of foliage plant possibilities, these three shine with stellar proportions in shade.

Fern Hardy ferns grow 1 to 4 feet tall and thrive in varying shade, especially if given enriched, well-drained, damp soil. Hardiness varies by species.

Coralbells The genus *Heuchera* includes a kaleidoscope of leafy colors, forms, and tinted patterns. Plant in sun to part shade.

Hosta Prized for their array of leaf colors, sizes, and textures, hostas flaunt flowers, too. Use these versatile shade plants as accents or en masse.

left, top This scheme includes hostas, ferns, and browallia along with sedge, goatsbeard, and deadnettle.

CREATE COLORFUL COMBINATIONS

If you're unsure about trying a new plant combination, gather a leaf from each of the prospects and get a clearer picture of how they will work together. At the nursery or garden center, group potted plants in a shopping cart to see whether they create a satisfying effect.

Foliage patterns enable you to contrast leaf sizes—from the tiniest of groundcovers to the massive lobes of tropicals—and overall plant forms. Foliage challenges you to see how it illuminates shady spaces. Choose leaves with silver, bronze, or another metallic hue to reflect light and act as surprising unifiers when repeated in the garden. Explore the gamut of greens, from chartreuse to blue-green, plus purple, orange, and other leaf colors.

STUNNING FOLIAGE

The leafy portion of plants plays a larger role in gardens than many realize. On the other hand, hostas, ornamental grasses, and other foliage families are the stuff of many plant collectors' dreams. Whether you're well acquainted with their finer qualities or not, these are a few favorites from the leafy realm.

1. BUGLEWEED (*Ajuga*) Quick-growing varieties create a dense mat. Flower spikes form on low-growing leaves in part sun to shade; Zones 3–11.

2. CALADIUM (*Caladium*) The color-splashed foliage brings drama to shade throughout summer. These tropicals grown from tubers must spend cold winters indoors.

3. CANNA (*Canna*) These easy-to-grow tropical bloomers have large paddle-shape leaves and reach 4 to 10 feet tall. Dig and store the rhizomes indoors over winter. Zones 7–10.

4. DEADNETTLE (*Lamium*) Cultivated for its chartreuse or silver-variegated leaves with season-long color, this ground-covering perennial also blossoms in spring. Zones 3–9.

5. COLEUS (*Solenostemon scutellarioides*) Once limited to sun-averse varieties, this genus of extroverted tropical plants includes hybrids adapted to sun and shade.

6. MAIDEN GRASS (*Miscanthus*) Among the splendid ornamental grasses, this genus includes many pretty sprays from 4 to 6 feet tall with dramatic autumn plumes. Zones 4–9.

7. ORNAMENTAL KALE (*Brassica oleracea*) This colorful annual perks up plantings when temperatures tumble. It prefers sun to part shade and moist soil.

8. DUSTY MILLER (*Senecio cineraria*) A compact, bushy annual with silver leaves, it reaches 8 to 16 inches tall. There are several varieties with different leaf forms.

9. DRACAENA (*Dracaena*) Also known as corn plant or spike, this tropical has narrow arching leaves and varying forms. Some varieties have stripes.

Easy Spring-Flowering Bulbs

Plant hardy bulbs in fall to enjoy the beauty in spring. For best success, choose planting areas with well-draining soil that will receive plenty of sun in spring.

Hardy bulbs stay in the ground over winter and bloom in spring. Although tulips and daffodils are the hands-down favorites, many lesser-known delights await fall planting. You can plant up until the ground freezes, but it's better to give bulbs a chance to begin rooting by planting in fall after the soil has cooled to 40 to 50°F.

Naturalizing bulbs

Many bulbs will multiply and prosper for years—naturalize— if planted well. Plant drifts of a dozen or more bulbs under deciduous trees, in lawns, or in rock gardens. Planting bulbs in loose groups randomly placed, rather than in soldier-straight lines, creates a natural effect.

Follow these tips to plant bulbs successfully:

Choose bulbs suited to your region's climate.

Improve soil drainage by covering the bottom of the planting hole with gravel or sand.

Place a 2-inch tulip bulb at least 6 inches deep—pointed end up. The planting depth should be three times the bulb height.

Plant bulbs to bloom in natural-looking clusters. Randomly position groups of seven or more bulbs in planting holes with the points up.

Remove spent flowers, but allow foliage to ripen, turn yellow and brown, and wither before mowing or cutting it. The leaves provide food for the bulbs—and next year's flowers.

PLANT BULBS THE EASY WAY

1 DIG HOLES
Use a shovel or spade to dig planting holes big enough to hold a handful of bulbs.

2 PLANTING DEPTH
Plant bulbs three times as deep as their height. Shown: Species tulip bulbs planted 3 inches deep.

3 SPRINKLE GRAVEL
Protect bulbs from hungry critters, especially if squirrels, chipmunks, and burrowing rodents are a problem in your region.

4 PROTECT BULBS
Another method of protecting bulbs from furry munchers: Enclose bulbs in hardware cloth or chicken wire.

5 COVER BULBS
Mark the planting area with a golf tee to avoid digging there.

right Ideal garden partners, crocus and narcissus bloom at the same time in early spring. **opposite, top** Tulips and narcissus are classic early spring bloomers. Choose varieties that bloom at the same time.

LONG-TERM VS. SHORT-TERM BULBS

LOW-MAINTENANCE GARDENING TIP

Some hardy bulbs return each spring. Many varieties of daffodils, scilla, and species tulips naturalize (multiply and spread) on their own and last for decades. But some hybrid tulips, hyacinths, and others are shorter-lived. They bloom for a year or two, then do not return again because the nutrients in the bulbs are depleted, causing the bulbs to decline in vigor.

FAVORITE HARDY BULBS

Among the easiest types of garden plants to grow, bulbs perform amazing magic with minimal attention. Bulbs planted in clusters and en masse make the biggest impression, so be generous when you plant. If you must store bulbs before fall planting time arrives, keep them temporarily in a cool, dry, dark place such as a basement.

1. ALLIUM (*Allium*) Long-lasting ornamental onions vary from low-growing star shapes to hip-high giant asterisks. Some are hardier than others.

2. CROCUS (*Crocus*) Signaling the end of winter, these bright and early bloomers rise 4 to 6 inches tall and shine year after year. Plant fall-blooming crocuses, too.

3. DAFFODIL (*Narcissus*) Countless variations trumpet spring with early- to late-season blooms: short or tall, bright or pastel, sweet scented or subtle, and more.

4. FRITILLARIA (*Fritillaria*) Species differ in size, color, and overall form, but all have bell-shape flowers. Each brings dramatic character to the garden.

5. TULIP (*Tulipa*) So many types, so little time to tiptoe through the early-, mid-, and late-season varieties. Hardy species tulips return for years most reliably and even naturalize.

6. GRAPE HYACINTH (*Muscari*) Blue, purple, or white grapelike flowers on 6-inch stems grow easily. Plant dozens of them to form exquisite drifts. They make good cut flowers.

7. HYACINTH (*Hyacinthus orientalis*) Few flowers can match the perfume of these stocky 6- to 10-inch bloom stalks. A range of color combines beautifully with other spring bloomers.

Easy Summer-Flowering Bulbs

Grace your garden with some of summer's most glorious flowers and lavish foliage.

Most summer-flowering bulbs are tender by nature and cannot survive cold winters without protection. Still, these exceptional plants are well worth growing.

In warm-climate zones, summer bulbs perform as perennials. At season's end in frosty areas, you can dig and save summer bulbs indoors over winter—or not. Grow them as annuals if you prefer. Or grow them in pots and winter the pots indoors.

However you grow them, summer bulbs are especially easy and rewarding. Plant once the weather is dependably warm, then wait for vibrant colors, bold textures, and sweet scents to develop. Summer heat encourages their performance. If summer is short in your area, start bulbs in a pot to get a head start on the growing season, then transplant into warm garden soil in late spring.

To protect summer bulbs from frost, gently dig and lift them with a garden fork or small shovel. Shake or brush off excess soil. Snip the remaining stems to 4 inches or so. Rinse the bulbs and let them air-dry for a few days. Pack the bulbs into a box of damp peat moss and store it away from heat and cold until spring.

In Pots In spring, plant lily bulbs in gallon pots and keep the soil damp. When plants develop and emerge from the soil, transplant them into the garden.

In the Ground In fall or spring, plant lily bulbs. When they bloom, fertilize the plants to encourage their return next year.

LOW-MAINTENANCE GARDENING TIP

PLANT LILIES IN SPRING AND FALL

Plant hardy lily bulbs in early fall (the preferred season) or spring in well-drained fertile soil and full sun. When plants emerge, spread mulch among them to help retain soil moisture.

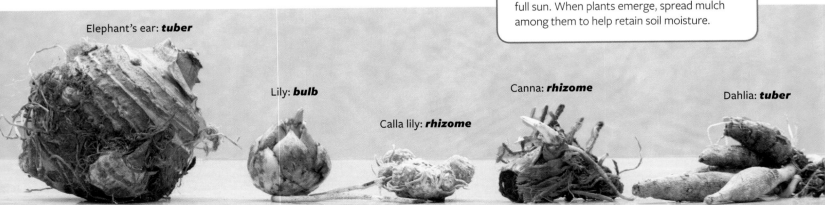

Elephant's ear: *tuber*

Lily: *bulb*

Calla lily: *rhizome*

Canna: *rhizome*

Dahlia: *tuber*

TYPES OF LILIES

Dazzling trumpetlike lily flowers are the backbone of a summer garden. Their heights range from 12 inches to 6 feet. Select varieties for a parade of blooms from June to September in well-drained, fertile soil and full sun: Asiatic hybrids (June and July), Martagon (June and July), Oriental hybrids (July and August), and Trumpet (July and August).

SUPER SUMMER BULBS

Summer bulbs grow from tubers, rhizomes, or tuberous roots as well as bulbs. Use the tropical look of the plants to your advantage, making a garden rendition of a favorite tropical vacation spot, complete with fragrant tuberoses, lush tuberous begonias, and nodding elephant's ears. Try different summer bulbs to find your favorites.

1. PINEAPPLE LILY (*Eucomis*) If you want to dazzle your friends, grow this South African native in a pot and enjoy its long-lasting pineapplelike blooms. Grow it in full to part sun; in gardens in Zones 7–10.

2. CANNA (*Canna*) Reaching 3 to 6 feet or more, this showy tropical has torchlike blooms and large sculpted leaves; colors depend on the variety. Cannas are hardy to Zone 7.

3. CALLA LILY (*Zantedeschia*) Colorful leaves (not flowers) unroll in white, yellow, hues of pink, and more. Grow in sun to light shade. The rhizomes are hardy to Zone 8.

4. ELEPHANT'S EAR (*Alocasia, Colocasia,* and *Xanthosoma*) The massive leaves dance on 3- to 6-foot stems in part sun or shade and create a tropical vibe. It's excellent in a pot or a water garden.

5. CALADIUM (*Caladium*) Grown for its flamboyant foliage, caladium grow to 30 inches tall. Some varieties require shade; others tolerate a few hours of sun daily. They're hardy in Zones 9 and higher.

6. DAHLIA (*Dahlia*) For drama in bold colors, choose from a range of bloom types and plant heights. Some need support. The tubers do best in rich, sandy loam. They're hardy to Zone 8.

After-Bloom Care

Removing spent flowers encourages many plants to rebloom and makes your garden appear neater, among other benefits.

Most annuals increase flowering after deadheading. Perennials that bloom on leaf-bearing stems also keep producing flowers when deadheaded. Cutting back some perennials, such as catmint, blanket flower, and geranium, promotes a second flush of flowers and a denser habit later in summer.

Snap off flowers with succulent stems that break easily or use pruners to cut withered stalks at their base. Remove only faded flowers, leaving buds to produce the next wave of blooms.

Some plants don't need deadheading. Attractive seedheads of ornamental grasses and other perennials can be left over winter to add interest to the garden. Also leave seedheads to develop if you want to collect seeds or let the plants self-sow.

The Show Goes On
Salvia splendens is one of the many annuals that benefit from deadheading. After deadheading, it reblooms within a couple of weeks.

LOW-MAINTENANCE GARDENING TIP

CHOOSE SELF-CLEANING PLANTS

Sterile plants that do not produce seed will bloom continuously without deadheading. More of these self-cleaning plants are being bred, including varieties of calibrachoa, petunia, lobelia, and bidens.

Time for Trimming
When blooms fade, turn brown, wither, or otherwise appear unattractive, it's time to trim them off.

Pinch or Cut
Sever the stem at its base, using a thumbnail or pruner to make a clean cut and avoid tearing the stem.

Next Up
Removing blooms signals new buds to develop. It also stimulates more profuse blooming.

NEATNESS COUNTS

Keep your garden looking its best with a weekly trim-up session. Removing faded flowers as well as dying plant material will keep your garden neat and healthy.

Flowering Finish Cut the stems of spent daffodils and other flowering bulbs. Leave the foliage to wither naturally and help feed next year's flowers.

Pinch an Inch Remove the tips of some plants (heliopsis, chrysanthemum, bee balm) in spring and early summer to maximize branching later.

Prolific Seedheads The flowers of some plants (garlic chives, columbine) develop seedheads and sow themselves with abandon unless you cut off the seedheads.

Soft Stems Pinch or snip a stem near ground level after the flower fades to promote new growth (pansy and other annuals, penstemon, veronica).

Tough Stalks Use sharp pruners to cut a stem just above a leaf or set of leaves or at the base of the flower stem (lily, peony, phlox).

Multiple Stems Shear the tops of plants with lots of small flowers (coreopsis, dianthus, shasta daisy) just above foliage level.

> **LOW-MAINTENANCE GARDENING TIP**
>
> ## REMOVE FADED FLOWERS AND FOLIAGE
>
> Deadheading (the process of removing faded flowers) promotes more continuous blooms among annuals and some perennials. In particular, it prevents the plants from producing seeds and extends their bloom cycle. If you don't deadhead annuals, they will most likely complete their life cycle sooner.

Easy Shrubs

By taking advantage of the versatility of shrubs, you'll make the best use of them in your garden. Plan for a continuous show and get the most impact from form, color, and texture.

Many shrubs have multiple strengths with a series of flowers, foliage, berries, and bark from season to season. When you consider shrubs for your garden, tally their seasonal strengths and identify the candidates with the most potential.

From the year's earliest witch hazel and winter daphne to the final hydrangea and rose of sharon, spring- and summer-flowering shrubs set the garden's pace. Beyond the color and fragrance that come with many flowers, compare the shrubs' type of blooms: large blowsy roses, fluffy spirea, dainty sweetspire.

Although a shrub's flowers may win your heart, select a plant first for its form (size and shape) and foliage. Foliage sustains the appeal of shrubs from season to season. Investigate the array of varieties with leaves other than standard green: chartreuse, blue-green, gray, and purple, for examples. Then consider shrubs that turn color and create brilliant autumn displays.

Berries that ripen in late summer or fall and last into winter can be a shrub's best feature because they attract and sustain birds. Planting berried shrubs brings life, color, movement, and song to your garden.

As leaves fall, the colorful bark and architectural forms of some shrubs bare of foliage take center stage to command the winter garden.

left top Evergreen shrubs create a lush year-round display and need little maintenance. **left bottom** The garden season begins with the beauty of flowering shrubs such as rhododendrons and their wafting fragrance.

SHOW OFF SMALL SHRUBS

LOW-MAINTENANCE GARDENING TIP

Use shrubs to make a small garden appear larger. Use light, bright broadleaf foliage at the front and darker, small-leaf varieties at the back to create an illusion of space. Choose slow-growing dwarf varieties here and there as focal points.

SHRUBS FOR ALL SEASONS

Shrubs demand less and give much more than most plants. When you choose shrub varieties with drought, disease, and pest resistance and amend the soil regularly, you'll minimize maintenance even more. These shrubs are among the most adaptive for a range of soils and climates.

1. CYPRESS, GOLDEN SAWARA THREADLEAF (*Chamaecyparis pisifera* 'Filifera') A slow-growing, mounding evergreen, this is favored as an accent plant for Zones 4–8.

2. DOGWOOD, RED-OSIER (*Cornus sericea*) Widely favored for its red stems in winter, the mounded shrub is good for hedges or in mixed borders in Zones 2–7.

3. ELDERBERRY 'BLACK LACE' (*Sambucus nigra*) With its dark foliage and contrasting flower clusters, this shrub adds a dramatic accent to a perennial border in Zones 4–7.

4. EUONYMUS (*E. fortunei* 'Emerald 'n' Gold') Use the compact, golden-variegated broadleaf evergreen as an accent or easy-care hedge plant in Zones 5–8.

5. INKBERRY (*Ilex glabra*) From the vast holly family, this upright, rounded, and slow-growing broadleaf evergreen likes damp soil in Zones 5–9.

6. JUNIPER, PFITZER (*Juniperus chinensis* 'Pfitzeriana') This spreading shrub reaches 3 to 5 feet tall and 6 to 10 feet wide; tolerates full sun and drought in Zones 4–9.

7. NINEBARK, PURPLE (*Physocarpus opulifolius*) This arching shrub has multiseason appeal: flowers, textured foliage, fruit, and colorful stems in Zones 3–8.

8. SPIREA, VAN HOUTTE (*Spiraea* × *vanhouttei*) Arching branches of this 6- to 8-foot spring bloomer bear white flower clusters in Zones 3–8. 'Bridalwreath' is ideal for hedges.

9. VIBURNUM (*Viburnum*) Consider this diverse group of shrubs with flowers, fruit, and stunning fall foliage for Zones 3–9. Some are evergreen, others deciduous.

This mixed border includes a dwarf burning bush along with perennials and ornamental grasses.

LOW-MAINTENANCE GARDENING TIP

ENSURE TREE AND SHRUB HEALTH

During the first year after planting, water is the most important factor in new tree and shrub survival. Ample water given occasionally is much better than shallow watering. Let the water trickle from a hose for 10 to 15 minutes on the soil surface beside the tree or shrub.

Planting Shrubs

Whether you plant a solitary selection, establish a privacy screen, or form a windbreak, plant shrubs with care, then protect your investment.

Although shrubs and trees cost more than other garden plants, their jobs are multipurpose and long-term. Container-grown or balled-and-burlapped shrubs cost more, but the well-developed roots usually establish quickly. The plants will mature within a few years. Bare-root and containerized plants will need more time and care to develop.

Get shrubs off to a good start, watering them weekly if needed through the first season. After that, they'll grow more independently and need only occasional pruning if they are damaged, misshapen, or overgrown. Mulch shrubs annually to preserve soil moisture, insulate roots from temperature extremes, discourage weeds, and gradually improve soil.

NEW SHRUB CARE

Provide young plants with basic care, then watch them succeed.

Postponed planting If you cannot plant right away, store potted and balled-and-burlapped plants in a cool, shady place away from direct sunlight and wind.

Ideal timing Spring, late summer, and early fall are the best times to plant shrubs. Avoid planting during the hottest part of summer.

Water adequately Water a new shrub deeply after planting, then weekly in the absence of rain throughout the first season.

Feed later New shrubs and trees do not require fertilizer the first year in the garden.

LOW-MAINTENANCE PLANTING

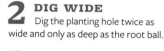

1 CHECK SPACING Measure the planting site and allow room for the shrub to reach full size.

2 DIG WIDE Dig the planting hole twice as wide and only as deep as the root ball.

3 REMOVE POT Slide the nursery pot off the root ball. Lift the shrub by the root ball into the planting hole.

4 FILL HOLE Backfill around the root ball, using leftover soil and sod to form a rim for watering.

5 MULCH AND WATER Cover the rim with a 2-inch layer of mulch. Keep mulch away from the shrub's trunk.

LOW-MAINTENANCE GARDENING TIP
BUY BARE-ROOT

If you want to save money or plant large quantities of shrubs, buy bare-root plants. Soak the dormant roots in a tub of water for several hours before planting.

Easy Roses

From the fleeting beauty of a single blossom to the lasting spectacle of a rose-draped arbor, there's a rose for any garden. Choose the best candidates for your place.

Adding roses to your garden entails the same practice of matching plant to site and conditions as any other shrub. The big difference is that there are so many different types and varieties of roses. How is it possible to sort out and explore the vast array of roses and find ideal options for your garden?

Consider the families of roses, from petite miniatures to massive climbers, and decide where you want to plant them. Then make a list of desirable varieties that you read and hear about. Prioritize hardiness for your region's climate and disease resistance. Choose roses on the basis of size, bloom color, name, introduction date, or whatever qualifications suit you. Some gardeners choose roses for their history or fragrance.

If you want the beauty of roses without the work often ascribed to them, you'll find an increasing selection of hardier plants. By growing different varieties, you'll see how easy roses can be. Buy own-root roses, grown from cuttings and cultivated on their own roots (not grafted onto a different rootstock), which are typically hardier and virus-free.

 CHOOSE FRAGRANT ROSES

Many heirloom roses boast exquisite fragrances, from sweet to spicy, fruity, musky, and more. You'll find many other fragrant varieties among David Austin, hybrid tea, and grandiflora roses. The scent of any rose is affected by climate. Fragrance is enhanced by mild humidity and warmth.

left An ever-expanding selection of modern roses, such as 'Lena' shrub rose, takes various forms, from neat bushes with a profusion of long-lasting flower clusters to tall arching and sprawling plants.

ROSE OPTIONS When buying roses, choose from bare-root, potted, or packaged bare-root plants. Look for green (not brown) bare roots and plant when they're dormant or just sprouting.

TYPES OF ROSES

Technically, roses are shrubs. But there are diverse families of roses, and varieties within those groups, which offer sizes, colors, shapes, and forms to suit every garden. The family of shrub roses includes some of the toughest, most pleasing ones of all. They're the choicest plants for 4- to 5-foot hedges or 6- to 8-foot screens. Meet some of the other rose families.

1. FLORIBUNDA This includes hardy 3- to 4-foot shrubs with profuse clustered flowers on short stems. Good for mixed beds and low hedges. Shown: 'Iceberg'.

2. GRANDIFLORA The shrubs reach 4 to 6 feet tall with abundant clusters of continuous blooms. Vigorous background plants for perennials. Shown: 'Earth Song'.

3. MINIATURE These diminutive treasures suit small spaces, pots, and bed edges. Some grow to only 6 inches; climbing varieties reach 8 feet. Shown: 'Caliente'.

4. HYBRID TEA The most widely grown rose type produces a large bloom on a single stem. Upright plants from 3 to 5 feet tall blossom repeatedly. Shown: 'Double Delight'.

5. OLD GARDEN The antique roses have survived generations with their rugged hardiness. Their flowers have delicate petals and dizzying scents. Shown: 'Harison's Yellow'.

6. CLIMBERS, RAMBLERS These large shrub roses with sprawling canes reach as tall as 15 feet. Give them strong support, such as a fence, wall, or pillar. Shown: 'New Dawn'.

7. SPECIES OR WILD These roses are the toughest; upright or low spreading and notoriously thorny. In late season, most have big hips (fruits). Shown: 'Frau Dagmar Hastrup'.

SELECT EASY-CARE ROSES

Roses with the Earth-Kind designation are tested and recommended for low maintenance, particularly for outstanding performance without the use of chemicals. The Texas A&M University program has inspired research in other states with other landscape plants.

Planting Roses

Proper planting gives your rose a sustainable foundation that helps protect the plant from the inevitable challenges of life in the garden.

The better health a rose has from its start in your garden, the better its chances of thriving. A well-planted, healthy rose is better able to fight off diseases and pests, reach out its roots to find water and food, and produce more leaves to help sustain the plant. Spring and fall are the best times to plant roses.

How deep to plant

Follow the steps below when planting any rose, whether bare-root, own-root, or containerized. The main difference is the depth at which to plant. To check the depth of your rose, lay a shovel handle across the planting hole and add or remove soil to adjust the planting level.

Plant own-root roses with the crown (where the main stem and roots meet) at ground level. In cold climates, set the crown 2 or 3 inches below soil level for extra winter protection.

Some bare-root or containerized plants have a graft union (a swollen knobby part of the stem just above the roots) where a desirable rose was grafted onto the roots of a more vigorous rose to combine the best of two plants. The graft union can be easily damaged by cold, so plant the graft union 1 to 4 inches below the soil level in cold-winter regions. In climates where winter temperatures do not drop regularly below 10°F, the graft can be planted at soil level or an inch above.

LOW-MAINTENANCE PLANTING

1 SOAK ROOTS
As soon as you get a bare-root rose, carefully remove it from any packing material. Soak the roots in a bucket of water for several hours.

2 PRUNE LIGHTLY
Snip off any damaged branches and roots. Your rose needs as many healthy roots as possible to reestablish itself once planted.

3 DIG A HOLE
Make the hole at least twice as wide as the root system. Work in soil amendments, such as compost or peat moss, as you dig.

4 SET ROOTS
Gently spread the roots in the bottom of the planting hole. Backfill to eliminate air pockets and keep the plant from settling too low.

5 WATER DEEPLY
Finish backfilling the planting hole. Mound and shape a moat of soil around the plant. Fill the moat with water. Let the water soak in; water again.

LOW-MAINTENANCE GARDENING TIP

GROW CONTAINER ROSES

Almost any rose can be grown in a container. Select a pot that provides plenty of rooting room: a 10- to 15-gallon pot for most roses. Use a larger container for larger roses; a smaller pot for miniatures.

opposite Apply a 2- to 3-inch layer of shredded bark, chopped leaves, or another organic material every season to prevent weeds and retain soil moisture.

Easy Vines

The sky's the limit when you incorporate vines into your garden. Choose from annuals or perennials—or both—to get the effects you desire.

You'll find an array of vines with individual strengths and rewarding ways to grow them. First, consider the broad categories.

Annual vines live only for one growing season, but their quick growth provides abundant color that can be changed easily each year. Although many annual vines put on a show in record time, they'll be felled by frost or the season's eventual end.

Easy-care perennials live on, adding character year after year. Once planted, most vines fend for themselves, needing only occasional trimming. Climbing plants tend to be tough, seldom fussy about soil, and resistant to most diseases. Many are drought-tolerant and produce week after week of bloom.

Trimming is good

If you trim spent flowers from annual vines, you'll promote new blooms. Some perennials, such as trumpet creeper and wisteria, can grow quickly out of control unless disciplined by regular pruning back.

Flowering perennials should be trimmed right after blooming to give next year's flowers maximum time to develop. If your vine has fruiting potential, stand back and wait as flowers give way to berries.

left Climbing rose and royal trumpet vine (just beginning to bloom) shelter a sunny sitting area. Strong wire trellising keeps both plants upright.

LOW-
MAINTENANCE
GARDENING
TIP

MIX PERENNIAL WITH ANNUAL VINES

Many perennial vines and climbers take two or three years to establish and commence flowering. In the meantime, complement them with annual vines that will bloom in their stead.

EASY-GROWING ANNUAL VINES

Colorful flowers, an undemanding nature, and a remarkable capacity for fast growth make an annual vine an asset in a garden. Most annuals grow easily from seeds; some can be sown directly in warm garden soil. Annual vines weigh less than woody perennials and require less support. Pruning is usually unnecessary. Fertilize in spring and early summer to promote fast growth.

1. BLACK-EYED SUSAN VINE (*Thunbergia alata*) Grow this 6- to 8-foot twiner from seed and enjoy the bright color blooms from midsummer on. It's an excellent container plant.

2. CARDINAL CLIMBER (*Ipomoea × multifida*) The 10- to 15-foot twining vine with delicate foliage and scarlet flowers lures hummingbirds. It needs well-draining soil.

3. CANDY CORN VINE (*Manettia inflata*) This unusual 6-foot-tall bloomer is also known as firecracker plant. Easy to grow in a pot, it attracts hummingbirds and butterflies.

4. HYACINTH BEAN VINE (*Dolichos lablab*) Growing rapidly to 15 to 30 feet, this showy twiner has purple flowers, foliage, and seedpods. Contrast it with silvery blue plants.

5. MANDEVILLA (*Mandevilla × amabilis*) A tropical treat for Zones 10 and 11, it grows elsewhere in containers. Show off the summerlong blooms on a patio or sunny porch.

6. MORNING GLORY (*Ipomoea tricolor*) Blooming in a range of colors, this sun-loving twiner grows up to 10 feet tall. The flowers open in the morning and close by afternoon.

7. SCARLET RUNNER BEAN (*Phaseolus coccineus*) This 15-foot twiner, with bright red flowers and large edible beans, needs ample support, sun, and moisture.

8. SWEET PEA (*Lathyrus odorata*) Known for its fragrant, colorful flowers, the 6-foot vine climbs via tendrils and makes a fantastic hedge or screen, especially in cool climates.

9. SWEET POTATO VINE (*Ipomoea batatas*) Known for its fragrant, colorful flowers, the 6-foot vine climbs via tendrils and makes a fantastic hedge or screen, especially in cool climates.

Easy Vines

COMBINING VINES WITH STRUCTURES

Put vines to work, pairing them with sturdy support that match the weight and strength of the vine. Twiners such as honeysuckle or trumpet creeper may please you at the outset on a wooden trellis, but they will soon advance from tender shoots to very strong cords, then to wrist-size woody stems with enough weight to topple anything but the strongest iron posts or similar structure.

Better Fences
Cucumber, one of many climbing edibles, teams beautifully with vintage iron fencing.

Over and Above Arches and arbors, small or large, form simple frames such as this one for Malabar spinach in a container garden.

Quick Privacy Sturdy, lightweight bamboo makes a long-lasting trellis for Virginia creeper or other fast grower.

Pole Jumpers A trumpet creeper hides an unsightly pole, but the vine must be cut back annually to keep it in check.

Upwardly Mobile Plant a vine such as clematis at the foot of an obelisk or other upright structure, giving it support from the onset.

Disguise an Eyesore
A cloak of sweet autumn clematis turns an old shed into an attractive storage area.

PERENNIAL VINES

As well-established fixtures in your garden from year to year, perennial vines add color, texture, and fragrance to the setting. Pair a perennial vine with a strong structure that can support the plant for many years. Some perennial vines take a year or two to settle in and take off. Prune plants every year to remove dead wood and manage them.

1. TRUMPET CREEPER (*Campsis radicans*) This fast-growing twiner with showy flowers attracts hummingbirds in Zones 4–9. Prune yearly to control it.

2. HONEYSUCKLE (*Lonicera*) These twining deciduous or evergreen vines with fragrant flowers attract hummingbirds and butterflies. They can become invasive.

3. JASMINE (*Jasminum*) Different types add enchanting fragrance to a garden with white flowers in summer. Hardiness varies. Grow in a pot in cold climates.

4. HYDRANGEA, CLIMBING (*Hydrangea anomala petiolaris*) Clinging by rootlets, it prefers some shade and reaches 30 to 50 feet in Zones 4–8.

5. BITTERSWEET, AMERICAN (*Celastrus scandens*) The woody twiner fruits in fall when a male and female vine are planted. Avoid invasive Oriental bittersweet.

6. PORCELAIN BERRY (*Ampelopsis brevipedunculata*) Climbing via tendrils, this weedy vine has lobed, sometimes variegated foliage and showy berries in Zones 4–8.

7. HOP, COMMON (*Humulus lupulus*) In Zones 5–8, this vigorous twiner grows 10 to 15 feet in a season. Ornamental 'Aureus' has showy chartreuse foliage.

left Edible plants create a beautiful garden full of colorful, textural treats. This plot includes tomato, sunflower, potato, calendula, purple basil, and signet marigold. **above** Mix flowers and vegetables for an ornamental bed. Here, kohlrabi (a cousin to cabbage) and petunias (edible) in varying hues of purple celebrate a favorite color. **below** Whether you start from seeds or seedlings, vegetable gardens pay dividends quickly with fresh produce within a few weeks.

LOW-MAINTENANCE GARDENING TIP

START VEGGIE SEEDS INDOORS

One way to decide which plants you'll raise from seeds is the number of days required for plants to reach maturity. If the growing season is short where you live, start long-season plants from seed, including Brussels sprouts, eggplant, melon, pumpkin, tomatillo, and some tomatoes.

Easy Vegetables

From earth to table, nothing tastes as fresh as homegrown vegetables. Decide what you like to eat, then get growing. Combine vegetables, flowers, and herbs for a garden that's a feast for the palate and the eyes.

When it comes to weighing which vegetables to plant in your garden, the choice is obvious: Grow what you like to eat. Many vegetables are fun to grow, but if you cannot use all of the crops, share them with neighbors, friends, or a local food pantry.

Your garden size might place limitations on plant choices. Sprawling vines, such as pumpkins and cantaloupe, might need more room than an entire small garden can provide. For limited spaces and containers, select varieties developed for compact form and confined growth habits. Dwarf, patio, petite, and mini plants often yield full-size produce.

Plants or seeds?

Most gardeners grow only a few plants of each kind of vegetable and merely buy a four- or six-pack of plants at their local garden center. The price of that pack might be only a little more than the cost of a seed packet, and it saves the effort of growing the plants from seed.

Nonetheless, sowing seeds remains a key part of vegetable gardening for practical reasons. First, rapidly germinating vegetables, such as turnips, radishes, squash, corn, and beans, are generally easier to grow from seed planted directly in the garden. Second, seed companies offer far more varieties than you'll find for sale as seedlings, giving you more options. Besides, it's just plain fun to watch seeds germinate and grow.

When planting seeds, follow packet instructions regarding planting time, depth, and spacing. It's typical to plant more seeds than you need, then begin thinning (plucking out) excess seedlings after they develop several leaves.

Many gardeners relegate vegetables to one section of the yard and flowers to another. But the most striking gardens are often those that mix edible and ornamental plants to create beautiful and bountiful results in any size space. This works even better when you include varieties of edible plants that offer more ornamental qualities than standard types.

Ornamental edibles

Many gardeners relegate vegetables to one section of the yard and flowers to another. But the most striking gardens are often those that mix edible and ornamental plants to create beautiful and bountiful results in any size space. This works even better with varieties of edible plants that offer more ornamental qualities than standard types.

From functional to fabulous

Most vegetables thrive with the same care as flowering plants. But when you plan and plant your garden, select edible plants for aesthetic as well as practical reasons. Select varieties for size, form, color, and texture. Mingle purple-leaf basil and feathery dill with glossy broccoli and your favorite flowers. Choose from a paint box of colorful lettuces, chard, peppers, and eggplant. When tucked into beds, they'll add to the display.

Think creatively when working ornamentals into your garden design. Take advantage of the range of plants from ground-covering herbs to towering Jerusalem artichokes. Plant climbing beans and vining tomatoes on handsome supports as eye-catching vertical elements. Grow edible flowers such as pansies to add color to fresh greens. Enhance a perennial bed with the dramatic large leaves and buxom forms of rhubarb and summer squash.

Planting Vegetables

How you plant is as important as the varieties you choose. There are numerous ways to make the most of available gardening space.

Traditional rows are easy to cultivate, manage, and harvest. Gardeners have long planted vegetables in rows because deciding where to plant each crop influences how the garden grows overall.

For example, plant tall crops, such as corn and pole beans, on the north side of the garden to keep them from shadowing shorter crops or on the south side if you want to cast intermittent shade on shorter, heat-sensitive crops.

Spacing between seeds and rows depends on what you plant. As a general rule, follow the guidelines on the seed packet for best results. Large plants, such as squash and eggplant, need rows at least 3 feet apart and should be spaced 30 inches apart in the row. Smaller plants, such as onions and radishes, can tolerate rows 8 to 9 inches apart and can be planted 2 to 4 inches apart.

Wide-row planting makes efficient use of space, instead of giving up space to paths between narrow rows of plants. It allows you to plot the planting space in a densely planted grid and works well for greens, radishes, carrots, and beets.

Succession planting allows you to plant two crops efficiently in the same space, pairing a short-season crop that comes and goes before the longer-season crop develops and needs more growing room. For example, plant seeds of spinach and beets at once. By the time the spinach crop is gone, the beets will have begun to fill in the voids.

LOW-MAINTENANCE GARDENING TIP
GO VERTICAL

Be creative and make use of often-underutilized space: Just grow up. Save precious ground in a small garden by using trellises, stakes, and fencing to train vining crops such as pole beans, tomatoes, melons, and cucumbers.

Permanent Ink
Transform thrift-store silverware into plant markers that help you remember what you planted and where. Write on the handle, then plunge the long-lasting marker into the soil for a charming effect.

Spokes of lettuces include "cut and come again" varieties. Once cut, they continue to grow and provide more harvests.

LOW-MAINTENANCE VEGETABLE PLANTING TIPS

Better Transplants
Soaking the roots of seedlings in a liquid starter solution stimulates root growth so the plant can take off as soon as it is planted.

Space Savers Harvest more from a small garden by combining crops in the same area. For example, fast-growing radishes come and go, making room for a slower-growing crop of broccoli.

Planting Partners
Small plants can be grown in the spaces between other plants. Bushy, low-growing parsley fills in among caged tomato plants.

Pleasing Pots Some edibles, such as sweet potato vine, grow well in containers, a good option for small spaces and urban gardeners. Water potted edibles consistently.

Planting Grids As this raised bed layout demonstrates, any given plot will hold more plants when arranged in a grid pattern rather than rows. Tuck one or more plants into each square, depending on size.

Heaping Hills Some plants, such as summer squash and cucumber, adapt best when planted in hills because the soil drains especially well. Mulch to keep the heaped soil from drying out.

LOW-MAINTENANCE GARDENING TIP

AVOID DISEASE WITH ROTATION

Vegetables from the same families are often susceptible to the same pest and disease problems. To minimize problems, avoid planting closely related vegetables in the same spot for at least 3 years. Rotate plants in the same family—tomato (pepper, potato, eggplant), cabbage (broccoli, cauliflower, kohlrabi, kale, collards), and squash (cucumber, melon, pumpkin)—to different locations.

Growing Tomatoes

The must-have summer crop is not difficult to grow. Use this planting advice to spur your success.

Which type of tomato and which varieties will you grow? It depends on the amount of space you have and how you plan to use the fruit: fresh for salads and eating out of hand, in cooking, or preserving for later use. Stagger your crop with early and late varieties. Opt for disease-resistant varieties.

Determinate tomatoes Ideal for containers, these varieties grow into bushy plants that need little more than a stake for support. The uniform, limited crop develops in a condensed period of weeks, often early. Tall, heavy plants benefit when supported by a stout stake.

Indeterminate tomatoes The continually vining plants produce an unlimited stream of flowers and fruit throughout the season until frost. Keep indeterminate tomatoes upright by surrounding them with heavy-duty wire cages or use your favorite tomato support system.

When buying seedlings, choose healthy plants that show no signs of flowering or yellowing leaves. At planting time, use red mulch, a plastic sheeting that benefits tomato plants by warming soil, suppressing weeds, conserving water, and improving fruiting.

Keep plants healthy by allowing ample room between them for air circulation. Water regularly at the base of plants to avoid wetting leaves and feed with liquid plant food. Spread a 4-inch layer of organic mulch between plants.

LOW-MAINTENANCE GARDENING TIP
AVOID CRACKING AND SPLITTING SKINS

Cracking can be caused by wide fluctuations in temperature and moisture. Watering deeply each week and mulching help prevent cracking. Rapidly growing fruit is also susceptible to cracking. Avoid using excess fertilizer.

LOW-MAINTENANCE PLANTING
Follow these easy steps to plant tomatoes.

1 PREPARE SHEETS Cut the plastic mulch into a 2- to 3-foot square for each plant. Cut an X opening large enough for your hand and tomato seedling to fit through.

2 PINCH BRANCHES Remove a seedling's lowest leaves. Then bury the stem to the lowest remaining branch to encourage more-vigorous root growth.

3 PLANT THE TOMATO Small bush varieties should be planted 2 feet apart. Larger varieties, especially sprawling plants, need at least 3 to 4 feet of growing room.

4 FEED THE SEEDLINGS Give tomato plants a big gulp of good nutrition with a serving of fish emulsion.

5 SET THE CAGE Set the plant support in place. If you try to stake a plant later when it is larger, you might damage tender stalks.

TOMATO-GROWING TECHNIQUES

You'll need to stake, cage, or trellis some tomato plants.

Indeterminate vining plants grow lush and rangy, requiring you to tie them to stakes or support them with heavy-duty wire cages. Alternative supports, such as bamboo trellises, also work. Coax plants to grow within a support; prune them occasionally if need be.

Tomato Cage Heavy fruits are enough to topple a tomato plant under its weight. Give plants ample support by setting a tomato cage in place as soon as you plant.

Fencing Vines A vining cherry tomato plant climbs a fence with a little help. A cage supports the base of the plant while garden twine secures extended branches in ascent.

Choice Variety 'Maskotka', a tumbling-type cherry tomato, grows happily in a large bowl-shape pot or basket. The plants spill over the sides and need no additional support.

HARVESTING TOMATOES

Tomatoes reach their peak of juicy, tangy flavor when their color develops fully, but you can also pick fruit as soon as it shows a hint of color.

Ordinarily, when you pick ripe tomatoes, you keep them at room temperature out of direct sunlight until you're ready to eat them. Avoid chilling tomatoes in the refrigerator, where the cool temperature breaks down flavor and texture.

By the time the end of the garden season rolls around, you'll want to grab the crop while you can. Before the first frost takes the last of those precious tomatoes, harvest green fruit and use it as is or save it for later—enjoy fresh tomatoes long after you put your garden to bed.

Read All About It Wrap green tomatoes in newspaper and allow them to ripen in a cool place such as a basement. Check the tomatoes periodically and use the fully colored fruits.

At Season's End Set not-quite-ready tomatoes on a windowsill to finish ripening. At this stage, flavor will continue to develop in the fruit.

All-Star Veggies

Here's a taste of some of the most popular vegetable crops. All are widely adapted and easy to grow. But don't stop here. Explore a world full of wonderful varieties whose flavors, colors, and tolerance to growing conditions vary widely. Find the veggies best suited to your taste and garden.

Collect baskets of homegrown produce from your garden from spring through fall.

Asparagus Long-lived asparagus sends up spears for weeks each spring. Work composted manure into the soil between plants annually.

Bean, green Bush beans grow knee high; pole beans vine up to 6 feet with a sturdy trellis. Consider dried and shelling bean varieties, too.

Beet Valued for their sweet roots and earthy-tasting greens, beets grow easily from seed. Choose from red, yellow, white, and striped varieties.

Broccoli Easy to grow and packed with nutrients, this cool-weather crop will bolt and go to seed when hot weather arrives.

Carrot This crunchy, nutritious, and sweet root grows especially well in cool weather. Grow it in sandy, damp soil and raised beds.

Cucumber Productive plants grow easily in rows, beds, containers, or hills. Limit the quantity of plantings unless you plan to make pickles.

Cabbage Harvest the leafy heads in spring or fall. The root stub left behind may produce more tiny heads. Protect plants from cabbage butterflies.

Greens Rich in colors and nutrients, leafy Swiss chard, collards, kale, and other frost-tolerant crops grow easily and beautifully.

Lettuce Leafy varieties, in hues from chartreuse to purple, grow easily. Sow seeds in early spring and fall; stagger plantings for a continual harvest.

Melon Heat-loving melons hide under rambling, leafy vines. The plants need ample space, nutrients, and water to grow and produce well.

Eggplant Start seeds early; plant seedlings after the last frost date. Eggplant grows best during periods of high heat and humidity.

Onion, Leek, and Garlic The members of the onion family grow in any garden. Plant in full sun and in soil high in organic matter.

Pea Shell, snow, and snap peas are among the spring garden's treasures. They all thrive in full sun to part shade and well-drained soil.

Pepper Harvest sweet or hot peppers when they're green or let the fruit ripen to full flavor and color, whether red, yellow, orange, or purple.

Potato Plant in early spring, starting with seed potatoes from a garden center or mail-order source. They're easy to grow in a roomy container.

Tomato Tomatoes thrive on heat, grow in almost any soil, bear abundantly, and need a long season in which to mature.

Squash Summer squashes (zucchini, yellow, scallop) produce generously. Winter varieties include acorn, butternut, and spaghetti.

Harvesting Vegetables

When your vegetables reach peak flavor, it's time to pick a peck. Harvest time in the garden means you'll have the freshest flavors at the table.

Because vegetables mature at different rates, the advice is to pick each crop at its prime. Most crops reach peak flavor when they're young and tender. As vegetables and fruits pass maturity, they can become fibrous, tough, or rotten.

It's up to you to learn when a fruit or vegetable has reached its optimum harvest time. This might mean picking asparagus and tomatoes daily; eggplant and lettuce every few days. Harvest ripening peas and pole beans every couple of days to promote ongoing production over the season.

Eat or store freshly picked produce promptly. If you allow vegetables to sit on a counter for days, they lose moisture and vitamin content. The sugars in some crops, such as corn and peas, begin turning to starch unless the produce is refrigerated swiftly. To prevent vegetables from continued ripening, put them in a plastic bag in a refrigerator or cool, dark basement.

Carry a basket during garden strolls and you'll be equipped to bring in a load of ready produce.

PICK AT THE RIGHT TIME

The time of day when you pick the garden's bounty is important. For most fruits and vegetables, early morning is best for harvesting because that's when produce contains maximum sugars. Pick produce right after the dew dries.

left top Place harvested vegetables in a flat-bottomed trug or in a shallow bowl so veggies aren't crushed under the weight of the harvest.
left bottom Harvest time provides sweet rewards for backyard gardeners, in fruits as well as special moments.

HARVEST TIPS

No magical date on the calendar signifies harvest time. Depending on what you plant and when, you may harvest vegetables for several weeks—even months. Keep these tips in mind to get the most from your crops.

Lettuce Pinch or snip the plants' outer leaves or an entire head. Leafy cut-and-come-again varieties will grow back if you leave an inch or so of plant when cutting.

Radish Pull the mature roots as soon as they're big enough to enjoy. Radishes left in the ground too long can crack, become woody, and develop an unpleasantly hot flavor.

Garlic Plant in the fall and harvest the following summer when at least half the leaves have begun to yellow. Cure bulbs by hanging them in a warm, airy, shaded place for several weeks.

Carrot Bigger is not always better. Harvesting these vegetables while they are small means capturing a sweeter flavor; larger carrots often taste bitter and may be woody.

Broccoli When the head is fully developed and the flowers are tightly budded, use a knife to cut the stem about halfway down. The stalk will continue to produce side shoots.

Sweet Potato Root crops such as sweet potatoes can be harvested any time they are ready. Gather them before a heavy frost or freeze occurs that can damage the crop.

Cherry Tomato These wee fruits, along with grape- and currant-type tomatoes, are ready to pick and eat when fully colored. Snip the entire cluster if you like.

LOW-
MAINTENANCE
GARDENING
TIP

REGULATE THE TEMPERATURE

Remove coverings on warm or sunny days to keep from baking your plants. Most coverings are effective only at temperatures above 20°F. Tender plants may need protection from wind and hail, in addition to potentially damaging temperatures.

Most garden row cover fabrics are lightweight enough to drape directly over a crop. Pulled over wire supports, the fabric forms a tunnel and holds warmth.

Extending the Season

Stretch the growing season—in early spring and late fall—with these ideas for protecting plants from cold weather.

Most vegetable gardeners agree: The warm sun of late spring and early summer arrives too late and frost comes too early. While most vegetables require high temperatures and plenty of sun to grow, ripen, and produce, the growing season doesn't need to be limited by first and last frost dates.

The most effective way to extend the season is to protect seedling or maturing crops from frost, which usually entails some kind of covering. There are several ways to warm the soil around plants, from inexpensive products to freebies from a recycling bin. One of the most popular options is the cold frame, a bottomless box with a hinged clear plastic or glass lid.

In the spring, a cold frame allows the gardener to get an earlier start on the gardening season, nurturing seedlings in the protected environment. Whether you start seedlings yourself or purchase them from a greenhouse, a cold frame provides a good temporary home until planting time.

In fall quick-maturing vegetables, such as lettuce and greens, may be planted in cold frames from mid- to late summer for fall harvests. A cold frame can be set in the garden to shelter leeks, beets, and cabbages, allowing them to survive well into winter. For added protection in harsh climates, gardeners insulate cold frames with bales of hay around the perimeter.

PROTECT FROM EXTREME HEAT

Although temperature concerns often focus on season extension and protecting plants from cold, modifying temperatures in hot climates can also be beneficial. Create a shade screen to keep soil cooler and protect plants from sunscald and drying winds. Shade can extend the season for cool-weather crops, slowing them from bolting and developing bitter flavor during hot weather.

LOW-MAINTENANCE SEASON EXTENSION

Stretch the growing season on both ends by using some of these weather-defying tips.

COLD FRAME
Make a shelter for seedlings by hinging an old window sash to a wooden frame. Ventilate the box on sunny days by propping open the lid.

MILK JUG
Cut out the bottom of a plastic jug and use it as a protective cloche, similar to a mini greenhouse, for young plants. Wiggle the cut end of the jug into the soil.

WALL OF WATER
Water-filled tubes give off energy that warms the air and ground around a plant, giving it an earlier start.

FABRIC COVER
Drape low plants with lightweight garden fabric to insulate plants from frost. Use rocks here and there to keep the fabric in place.

Easy Herbs

Herbs reward with distinct scents and fresh flavors, whether you grow them in garden beds or containers, outdoors or indoors.

Most herbs grow as abundantly in containers as they do in garden beds. Work with the space you have and design a formal or informal scheme, an entire landscape, a plot outside the kitchen door, or a handy indoor windowsill garden.

Most herbs are as ornamental in the garden as they are useful after harvest. Those with flowers, such as chives, rosemary, and lavender, are attractive in their own right. Others have handsome foliage that pairs well with other plants in the garden. For example, purple-leaf basil contrasts nicely with leaf lettuce, and the wispy foliage of dill or fennel makes a soft background for sun-loving flowers such as roses.

Herbs, no more difficult to grow than vegetables or flowers, are hardy and rarely succumb to diseases and pests. Most herbs need little more than fertile soil with good drainage and regular weeding. Frequent harvesting of leaves keeps plants growing as lushly and productively as possible throughout the growing season.

Getting started
Herbs that grow easily from seed include basil, cilantro, and dill. Some start better as seedlings, including rosemary, French tarragon, and bay.

If you want just a couple of plants of each herb, start with seedlings in the spring. When buying herbs, check the botanical name to be sure you get the plant you want. Smell an herb and take a nibble to learn about its flavor and intensity.

left top Combine herbs with other edibles or flowers. This bed features potatoes, tricolor sage, purple basil, and signet marigolds.
left bottom A potted garden holds trailing nasturtium 'Gleam Yellow', French thyme, tricolor sage, and curly parsley—pleasing to the nose, eyes, and palate.

HERBS TOLERATE POOR SOIL

Many herbs are tough plants that can withstand various conditions. But they will grow more vigorously if planted in good-quality, well-draining soil, loaded with organic amendments. Go light on fertilizer, which encourages soft, cold-sensitive growth that has less fragrance and flavor.

EASY HERBS

Here's a taste of some of the most popular herbs. Most are exceptionally productive, contributing fresh flavor to foods from spring through fall. All are widely adapted and easy to grow. But keep looking. The world is full of wonderful varieties with unlimited flavors, colors, and tolerance to growing conditions.

1. BASIL (*Ocimum basilicum*) Pinch plant tips often to encourage branching and prevent flowers from forming. Harvest and use leaves fresh throughout the summer.

2. DILL (*Anethum graveolens*) Sow dill seeds directly in warm garden soil, planting every three weeks from spring until midsummer for a continuous supply of aromatic foliage.

3. LAVENDER (*Lavandula*) There are many varieties of this wonderfully fragrant herb. Add gravel to planting holes to give plants the well-draining conditions essential to their growth.

4. OREGANO (*Origanum vulgare*) The signature flavor in Italian cooking, this herb thrives in full sun and well-drained soil. It grows up to 2 feet tall. Use the leaves fresh or dried.

5. PARSLEY (*Petroselinum crispum*) For a steady supply of leaves, sow seeds in spring and midsummer. Curly-leaf parsley makes a frilly edging for garden beds.

6. CHIVES (*Allium schoenoprasum*) This perennial grows to 15 inches, with slender foliage and fluffy blooms. Harvest both and use them fresh or frozen for delicate onion flavor.

7. THYME (*Thymus*) Perennials, available in many varieties, need room to spread. Low-growing selections work well as garden edging or fillers between stepping-stones. .

8. SAGE (*Salvia officinalis*) Earthy and pungent, this woody evergreen perennial grows to 2½ feet. Harvest the leaves as needed and replace the plant after five years.

9. ROSEMARY (*Rosmarinus officinalis*) A tender perennial, rosemary grows into to a 2- to 4-foot-tall shrub. Snip side branches to encourage bushy growth.

Success with Herbs

Because of their beauty and wide range of size, shape, color, and texture, herbs offer a nearly limitless palette for the landscape.

Pay careful attention to the range of an herb's hardiness, its light and moisture requirements, and your region's last frost dates. All of these factors influence which herbs can grow successfully in your climate and where and how you raise them.

Most herbs will thrive with at least six hours of full sun daily. Many perennial plants, including thyme, rosemary, lavender, and sage, are native to the Mediterranean. They grow best in full sun and very well-drained, slightly alkaline soil.

Herbs don't need their own garden. Tuck them among vegetables and flowers for beautiful effects. Fit in a few basil plants among the tomatoes; replace spring pansies with cilantro. For a second crop of fast-growing annual herbs such as chervil and dill, plant seeds in midsummer to allow time for them to mature before the end of the growing season.

To get the most benefit and pleasure from growing herbs, make them a part of your everyday life, rather than something saved only for special occasions. In the kitchen, popular uses for herbs include making delicious pesto, flavored spreadable cheese, piquant salad dressings, and much more. Use them as aromatic garnishes for drinks and surprising additions to desserts.

Beyond their edible appeal, you can also use aromatic herbs around the house in fragrant bouquets and soothing body-care preparations. Growing herbs can lead you into a fascinating realm as you discover ways to use your plants.

left top Near the end of the growing season, transplant a few herbs, such as parsley and rosemary, into pots, then move them indoors to a sunny windowsill for the winter. **left bottom** Before herbs blossom, pinch off any buds. When harvesting herbs, stand fresh-cut stems in a glass of cool water and keep them handy for several days on the kitchen counter.

CLIP FRESH HERBS FOR COOKING

Strip fresh leaves off a stem by sliding your thumb and forefinger from stem top to bottom. Snip off larger leaves such as those of parsley that don't strip off readily; chop them just before adding to a dish.

Harvesting herbs

The more frequently you snip your favorite culinary herbs, the more densely they'll grow and continue producing. Cut stems from plants early in the day, after the dew has dried but before the sun bakes the plants' essential oils (the essence of flavor and fragrance). Harvest no more than one-third of the stem length and the plant will continue to produce throughout the season.

Herbs flourish in full sun. Integrate them into a kitchen garden, mixed border, or flowerbed. They adapt well to almost any spacious container, from a window box to patio pots.

HARVESTING HERBS

Snip and savor fresh herbs as often as possible. Near the end of the season, harvest plants and freeze or dry the leaves for extended use throughout the winter.

FRESH BASIL Harvest basil leaves as needed and pinch off any flowers that begin to form. Try varieties of basil and experiment with their flavors, from spicy to lemony.

NEAT AND TIDY Compact spicy globe basil forms a neat 8- to 12-inch edging plant. Shear plants often to maintain their low, mounding shape. The tiny leaves hold big flavor.

GOURMET FLOWERS Give fennel a place in the garden for its feathery foliage and licoricelike aroma. Gather the flowers and use their pollen in cooking.

PRETTY RISTRAS String spicy chiles, garlic, and sage for a decorative addition to the kitchen. Hang the ristra in a place away from light and heat to protect the flavors.

DELICIOUS DILL To keep dill producing tasty leaves, snip flowers as soon as they form. Cut the mature seedheads, dry them in a paper bag, and store the seeds in a jar.

STORING HERBS Once herbs are fully dried, the whole leaves can be stripped from the stems and stored in opaque containers away from light and heat.

CHAPTER SEVEN

Low-Maintenance Containers

Create beautiful easy-care gardens
in pots for patios and decks.

Benefits and Strategies

Do you dream of a beautiful garden but face constraints of time, energy, money, or space? Container gardening offers many ways to overcome limited resources.

Although contained plants rely on gardeners for their needs, you can devise a container-tending routine that's enjoyable and suits your everyday life. Before long, potted gardens will contribute to the daily use of your surroundings as well as the appearance of your home—indoors and outdoors.

Count on potted gardens to generate pleasure and make their setting more appealing. Containers are the ultimate garden accessories. They're colorful, portable, and changeable. Potted plantings encourage creative expression and reward it with cheerful displays that can extend the growing season, possibly going year-round.

Wherever you live, container gardens allow you to experiment with new plants and combinations. Containers enable you to enjoy plants that don't ordinarily grow in your location's climate or soil.

Wherever you put containers to work, they'll provide solutions—filling dull or bare spots, marking an entryway, creating privacy, decorating for a party, keeping produce handy, or adding flowery fragrance.

Indoors, you can turn windowsills, floors, and tables into garden spaces with a few plants. Plants add lush green life to any room and improve the air quality.

left Add sizzle to your decks and patios with colorful hot peppers.

Container gardening strategies

Practice strategic planting and use containers where they'll provide the most benefits. Versatile and portable, potted gardens can be staged to put on the best show.

As long as you give potted gardens adequate light, water, and food, they'll serve you well. Match plants to the available light conditions, whether growing single plants or grouping them. It takes only a few plants or pots to accomplish your mission.

Greet guests Framing an entryway or lining steps, containers soften the hard edges of architecture and create a welcoming vibe. They guide traffic when lining a walkway or make a small balcony seem more inviting.

Provide garden space Create a garden where there is not enough room or sun for a conventional one. Containers offer options for planting on a small patio, a stoop, or a sprawling deck or terrace. Potted plants add color and interest. In addition, containers place plants within comfortable or easy reach, such as growing edibles near a kitchen.

Use vertical space Where containers can hang or plants can climb, you'll make more efficient use of an area—and maybe even create more privacy in the process.

Unify the decor Employ a strategy most often used indoors, where repetition of color unites the decorating scheme. Use similar or identical containers or plants throughout an area to pull it together visually.

LOW-MAINTENANCE GARDENING TIP
MOVE HOUSEPLANTS OUTDOORS

Many plants, including an array of tropicals more commonly known as houseplants, can move outdoors for the summer and back indoors fall through spring. The plants create a vacationlike setting outdoors, then move back indoors healthier and stronger for the respite. Set plants in a shaded, protected place when you move them outdoors to help them adjust to stronger light.

MOVEABLE GARDENS

Growing plants in containers promotes gardening flexibility. Enjoy the color and texture of flowers and foliage indoors and out. Here's why container gardening is so popular.

GARDEN INDOORS
Group plants and pots with contrasting leaf shapes, colors, and textures, enlivening any room.

EASY DRAMA
Combine an edible plant (Swiss chard) with ornamental ones (tufted hairgrass and pansies) for a lasting show.

PICK A PEPPER
Raising fresh produce at a low cost adds to family meals throughout the growing season. Dwarf or compact varieties of peppers and tomatoes thrive in containers.

IVY LEAGUE
Growing in roomy planters and climbing on trellises, ivy forms a wall of privacy for a patio. Flowering plants add color; candles in staked holders create ambience after sunset.

Start with a Container

Selecting an ideal pot for your container garden helps ensure its success.

The best potted gardens start with well-chosen containers. Begin by matching the container to deliver enough space, moisture, nutrients, and air to nurture plants. The most-suitable containers also express the style of your home and garden.

Pick a pot

You'll find containers available in a huge range of types and materials, from classic terra-cotta and concrete to contemporary and self-watering planters. Synthetic pots (resin, plastic, fiberglass) last longer and shake off weather better than most natural types (wood, woven, fabric).

Colorful pots create instant garden accessories. Plain or decorative, lightweight or heavy, there are plenty of prospects available to suit any garden. Improvised containers also complement many garden designs. Picture an ornamental grass in a rustic bucket or an iron urn or a tall sleek cylinder—each metal container creates a different effect.

When choosing containers that appeal most to you, buy the best quality that you can afford. Balance the size of the container with the potential size of mature plants and their combined presence where you plan to place the garden. The larger the pot, the more room for roots and the slower soil dries. A shallow cast-concrete trough proves perfect for low-profile succulents, while a lightweight wall pot holds a precious begonia at eye level where you can notice it daily.

Good drainage is a container's most important feature. Unless a pot has a means of releasing excess water, plant roots can suffocate and die. If your pot doesn't have a drainage hole, use it as a decorative cachepot instead, holding a drainable pot inside it.

Glazed Alike
If you plan to group containers, select those with something in common, such as color or material.

Shape of Things
Big and deep (at least 12×12-inch) pots can host an assortment of plants and those with long or extensive roots.

By the Bushel
Gently used baskets or wooden crates work well to raise a veggie garden in a small space.

WEATHERPROOF YOUR CONTAINERS

Baskets, wooden crates, and other containers quickly disintegrate when exposed to continually wet soil and weather. Protect the exterior with several coats of waterproofing sealant. Plant in a plastic pot that fits inside the container.

The Anatomy of a Pot

Success depends on the container's ability to provide an adequate growing environment where roots can develop and flourish. All pots are not created equal. But good containers include essential characteristics that help plants thrive.

A. Clay Differences

Terra-cotta is reliable and easy to find. Unfired clay is heavy, rough-textured, and porous. It breaks more easily than high-fired clay. In a freezing climate, store pots in a sheltered place over winter.

B. Essential Moisture

Soil dries out faster in clay pots than in plastic or fiberglass ones. Large planters hold moisture longer than smaller ones.

C. Keep It Light

Lighten the weight of larger pots (more than 12 inches in diameter) to make them easier to move. An upside-down plastic pot or packing peanuts will do the job. Fill smaller pots with soil for good root growth.

D. Crucial Drainage

Pots must have a drainage hole for excess water to pass through. A saucer catches the water and helps prevent staining on a tabletop or deck.

MEASURE BEFORE YOU SHOP

Containers seem big enough at the store when you decide to purchase them. But when you bring them home, they appear smaller than the surroundings. Prevent this common problem by taking along measurements when shopping.

Planting a Container Garden

Think of a container garden as a miniature version of an inground garden. The goal is to make the finished container look good, fulfill its intended function, and help plants to thrive in a site you select.

Use a few guidelines and you'll be creating container gardens like a pro. Effective design starts with a container. Choose one that is aesthetically pleasing and practical. Think big to save time and effort. The bigger the pot, the less you'll need to water and the better your plants will perform.

Ready to plant

Choose healthy plants and a planting strategy. The simplest scheme includes a single variety or color. Combining different plants may entail balancing heights and forms with a tall star, a medium filler, and a trailing accent.

Group plants with similar needs for light and water. Grouping is accomplished with multiple plants in one container or with multiple containers in a pleasing arrangement. Mix foliage textures and bloom colors as you like. Choose long-blooming annuals or feature perennials, edibles, or houseplants.

Round up everything you will need for planting, including a clean container with adequate drainage. Choose a premium potting mix and other ingredients such as plant food based on the plants' needs for nutrients, moisture, and drainage.

Once planted, leave 2 inches between the top of the soil mix and the container rim for mulch (if desired) and water.

A note about the long-season container garden shown: The scheme features a shrub that can be transplanted into a garden bed in late summer or early fall. As a bonus, the variegated foliage plants can be transplanted into smaller pots, saved over winter indoors, then replanted in fresh container gardens for the next season.

LOW-MAINTENANCE GARDENING TIP

CHOOSE THE RIGHT PLANTS FOR YOUR POTS

First consider the size of the container, then determine the number of plants needed depending on nursery pot size and potential at maturity. When shopping for plants, set them on a cart to see how they might work together. When you take plants home, arrange them while in nursery pots at first. At planting time, adjust the positions in the container, considering how large the plants will grow.

EASY STEPS TO PERFECT POTS

1 GATHER ROUND
Plant a large container in place so you won't need to move it.

2 HALF-FILL POT
Snip off any damaged branches and roots. The plant needs as many healthy roots as possible to reestablish itself once planted.

3 FEED NOW
Sprinkle continuous-release plant food on the soil mix. This fertilizer will last for months.

4 ADD SOIL
Remove other plants from their nursery pots. Set them in place; fill in between with soil mix.

5 ALWAYS WATER
Sprinkle plantings thoroughly. Water as needed throughout the summer.

MIXING PLANTS IN A CONTAINER

Underplantings complement a young tree-form Quick Fire hydrangea (*Hydrangea paniculata* 'Bulk') in a 20-inch-diameter plastic pot. The grouping grows steadily, providing a lively display all season.

ANGELONIA
This sturdy annual blooms throughout summer if deadheaded consistently.

SCENTED GERANIUM
'Lady Plymouth', a rose-mint variety, has a pleasant fragrance and unique leaf shape.

SPIDER PLANT
'Variegatum' grows easily and adds a graceful accent to groupings.

SWEDISH IVY
This fast grower has trailing stems and a spicy scent.

Growing a Three-Season Garden

This potted garden goes with the flow, changes with the seasons, and epitomizes spring, summer, and fall with few changes.

Select a roomy pot, such as a 16-inch urn or the pot of your choice. Anchor the planting scheme with an upright evergreen tree or shrub that remains as the centerpiece throughout the growing season. The constant in this scheme is a golden juniper (*Juniperus communis* 'Gold Cone'), a dwarf variety that reaches 3 to 5 feet tall at maturity. Move it out of the pot and into the garden in fall.

Highlight it with annual flowers and foliage, first with a spring combo. Replace the annuals for a fresh display as spring turns to summer, then again as summer turns to fall. Use a dozen or fewer annuals in 3- to 4-inch pots to fill the planter each season. Relegate the passé plants to garden beds if you can't bear to compost them.

Keep a long-season container garden going strong by fueling it from the start: Plant with a premium potting mix that contains time-release plant food and moisture-holding granules or add these ingredients to your custom soil mix.

When changing the annuals, scoop them out of the pot using a trowel to avoid harming the shrub roots.

LOW-MAINTENANCE GARDENING TIP

KEEP A POTTED GARDEN GROWING ALL YEAR

If you live in a climate that allows it, grow plants in containers year-round for the most sustainable schemes. Many woody plants and hardy perennials will thrive in containers for several years in large enough pots. If freezing weather threatens the survival of potted plants in your region, transplant them to the garden in early fall and return them to the container the following spring.

Spring: Cool-Season Pastels

A. Ornamental kale
B. Verbena 'Quartz Waterfall Mix'
C. Stock
D. Viola

Summer: Warm-Season Changeouts

A. *Helichrysum petiolare* 'Lime Light'

B. New Guinea impatiens

Fall: Bright Replacements

A. Chrysanthemum 'Dawn'

B. *Liriope muscari* 'Variegata'

A new hanging basket looks lush from the start and fills out more during the season.

Planting a Hanging Basket

Take a simplified approach to assembling a beautiful hanging garden.

Garden centers commonly offer standard 10- or 12-inch hanging baskets. Although the plants are usually lush and beautiful, the plastic pots and hangers that come with them are not. Plenty of pretty woven-basket options also exist that give plants more growing space and create satisfying displays.

Hanging baskets often go on sale before summer reaches full swing, making this an economical container gardening idea. Planting is a breeze and a few tricks ensure success.

Ruffly petunias bloom and cascade and are ideal for hanging baskets and other containers. A sweet-scented, double-flowering variety puts on a colorful summerlong show. Monthly fertilizing keeps the show going strong.

LOW-MAINTENANCE GARDENING TIP
MINIMIZE HANGING BASKET WATERING

Start with the largest container possible to give plant roots room to spread. Added at planting time, two special materials available to gardeners make a difference: moisture-holding granules and a thick fabric-type basket liner. Then hang the basket where it will get needed light without baking in too much sun.

BUILD A BASKET

1 SET UP
Set 14-inch basket in a heavy pot to hold it. Remove the plastic liner.

2 BETTER LINER
Line the basket with moisture-holding fabric to let air reach plant roots.

3 ENRICHMENTS
Add fertilizer and moisture-holding granules to lightweight potting mix.

4 GET PLANTS
Release the plant root ball from the nursery pot, keeping it intact.

5 REPLANT
Set the root ball in the basket half-filled with potting mix. Fill in with more mix. Water.

Butterfly Garden Plant List

A. Butterfly weed 'Silky Deep Red'

B. Salvia 'Fuego'

C. Pineapple sage

D. Marigold

E. Pentas 'Ruby Glow'

F. Lantana 'Landmark Blaze'

G. Dill

H. Parsley

left Enjoy butterflies all summer when you plant a feast of nectar-producing and host plants. ***top*** A swallowtail butterfly is one of the garden's winged visitors.

Gardening in a Self-Watering Container

A container with a built-in water reservoir ensures plants receive consistent moisture while minimizing watering chores.

A self-watering container holds a limited water supply. Moisture is wicked to plant roots as the soil dries. You still need to water plants and refill the reservoir regularly, but less often, saving time and effort. Various self-watering containers are available.

The planter shown (40×17×32 inches) holds 100 quarts of potting mix and has built-in overflow drainage. Once the reservoir is full, excess water drains out, which is especially helpful after a rain.

Water Reservoir
Moisture is drawn up to the plant roots as needed.

Fill 'er Up
The water reservoir is refilled periodically.

BUTTERFLY GARDEN

Grow butterfly-friendly plants in a container garden on a deck or patio or in an opening in the garden where there is a need for color. Choose nectar-rich flowers, such as salvia, marigold, zinnia, and verbena, for your potted display.

1 MATERIALS READY
A rot-resistant cedar planter on legs allows you to garden without bending over.

2 PREPARE SOIL
Moisten a premium lightweight potting mix, blending until it's fluffy, not soggy.

3 ADD FERTILIZER
Mix slow-release plant food into the potting mix, following product suggested quantity.

4 FILL PLANTER
Add prepared potting mix to the planter within 2 inches of the rim.

5 ADD PLANTS
Ease one plant at a time out of its nursery pot, nestling its root ball into the potting mix.

6 WATER PLANTS
Water the soil mix to thoroughly moisten it and ensure root-to-mix contact.

LOW-MAINTENANCE GARDENING TIP

LURE BUTTERFLIES TO POTS

Consider the life stages of butterflies when choosing plants. They need places to lay eggs and form a chrysalis; leaves, stems, and buds for caterpillars to feed on; and nectar for adults.

Easy Plants for Pots

Most plants adapt to life in a container outdoors during the growing season. Single plants in single pots are easy to group effectively. Simplify plant combos by including only three elements—vertical, filler, trailer—for an effective design.

As you plan to plant a container garden and acquire plants, mix and match selections depending on garden conditions (sun, shade, or both) and goals. Depend on tried-and-true varieties or experiment with new and improved ones. Explore the array of plants particularly adaptable to life in containers.

Choosing plants for containers is as easy as picking up a flat of petunias at the garden center. You might shop with a color scheme in mind or just be drawn to delightful plants. Almost any plant can grow successfully in a container, at least for a limited time. Simplify the selection by focusing on plant strengths and the practical advantages they provide. Drought tolerance or slow growth is a bonus. You'll discover over time which plants are most rewarding for you.

Annual Color For a pot full of portable color, plant six Wave petunias in a lightweight 18-inch container. Apply liquid fertilizer every other week.

Bulbs for Spring As an early season treat, plant prechilled bulbs (available at garden centers) for a concert of daffodils, tulips, and grape hyacinths plus annual violas.

Evergreen Trio Dwarf evergreen trees and shrubs thrive year-round in spacious individual pots and form handsome groupings.

Delicious Duo Harvest spring lettuce, then let the 'Patio' tomato take over for summer pickings.

Fragrant Plants Favorite herbs, including lavender, basil 'Pesto Perpetuo', scented geranium, rosemary, and thyme, pack a planter with sensual delights

Perennial Fare Yes, you can grow perennials in containers. This one features gooseneck loosestrife and coralbells with lemongrass.

Simply Succulents A collection of young succulents prefers warm, bright light and careful watering (on the dry side).

Summer Show Canna and other summer-flowering bulbs grow well in a pot with annual accents (geranium, calibrachoa). Keep the bulb in the pot indoors over winter.

Houseplant Hiatus Give houseplants a summer vacation outdoors, where they'll thrive with filtered light, increased air circulation, and refreshing showers.

Rosy Reality A shrub rose blooms all summer as it grows in this deep container with annuals at its feet.

Vertically Inclined Pair a climber (black-eyed susan vine) with a trellis in a pot for a small-space solution. Annuals (calibrachoa, zinnia) add color.

Grassy Texture Even ornamental grasses do well in containers. Annual ruby grass teams with sweet potato vine for a marathon display.

CHAPTER EIGHT

Easy-Care Garden Plans

Create a minimal-care garden with customized problem-solving plans.

Drought-Tolerant Slope Garden

Overcoming erosion and other slope-related problems just got easier.
Tame a tough slope with this ultra-easy-care garden.

Mix and match plants; any type of low-growing sedum or thyme would
work in a sloping border such as this one.

Entry gardens really need to shine. If yours is on a slope, you may
find it physically challenging to maintain. Gardening on a slope
can stretch the backs of your legs to their limit and contort your
body as it tries to stay upright.

Multicolor sedum, thrift, and creeping thyme intermingle among
rough-hewn stone steps and jagged boulders in this hillside entry
garden. Colorful foliage draws visitors up the stairs to the front
door. If your garden center doesn't offer the sedum or thyme
specified in the plant list, substitute another. In regions where
New Zealand flax is not hardy, yucca or colorful shrubs such as
'Coppertina' ninebark (*Physocarpus* spp.) are just as effective.

Using low-care plants that thrive in full sun, warm weather,
and well-drained rocky, relatively infertile soil will help eliminate
that pain. Once settled in, low-care plants will survive on rainfall
and will need little deadheading or other hands-on care. Sedum
and thyme, for example, shed spent flowers; thrift requires only
one yearly deadheading.

Easy-care slopes

Solve slope problems by adopting a few simple strategies.

Choose rooty perennials Select perennials and shrubs that
thrive in dry soil and have dense, far-reaching root systems, such
as daylilies (*Hemerocallis* spp.) and California fuchsia (*Zauschneria*
spp.). Their roots form tight-knit mats to hold soil in place.

Use water-tolerant perennials Because water collects at
the base of slopes, choose plants for the bottom of the hill that
tolerate occasional wet feet.

Lay landscape cloth To prevent bare soil from eroding while
plants settle in, pin landscape cloth to the slope and cut slits in it to
plant through. Top with a layer of shredded bark mulch.

Water at ground level Use soaker hoses or a drip irrigation
system to ensure water moves into the ground rather than runs off.

PLANT LIST

A. 3 White stonecrop (*Sedum album* 'Chubby Fingers'): Zones 4–8

B. 5 Golden carpet sedum (*Sedum acre*): Zones 3–8

C. 1 Barrenwort (*Epimedium rubrum*): Zones 4–9

D. 6 Sea thrift (*Armeria maritima*): Zones 3–9

E. 4 Creeping thyme (*Thymus coccineus*): Zones 4–9

F. 1 New Zealand flax (*Phormium tenax*): Zones 8–10

G. 4 Hybrid sedum (*Sedum* 'Purple Emperor'): Zones 3–7

H. 1 Sea lavender (*Limonium latifolium*): Zones 5–9

I. 2 Oregon stonecrop (*Sedum oreganum*): Zones 2–9

J. 1 Two-row stonecrop (*Sedum spurium* 'Voodoo'): Zones 4–9

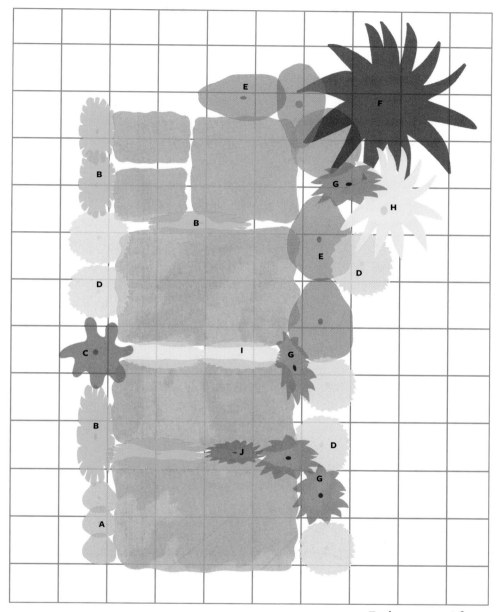

Each square = 1 foot

Springtime Splendor

A shady spot bursts into color every spring with a mix of blooming perennials, shrubs, and a showy Japanese maple as backdrop.

A dramatic garden has a focus, and you can hardly go wrong with Japanese maples. Most have exquisitely layered, cascading form; an elegant, fine leaf texture; and remarkable fall color. Among the many varieties available, you'll find maples with yellow-green, purple, red, bronze, or variegated leaves. And their sizes suit most landscapes, varying from 3-foot dwarfs to moderate 15-footers. Many Japanese maples have a wonderful way of spreading to become a low, graceful dome.

A mulched pathway borders a bed filled with colorful spring-blooming plants adapted to partial shade.

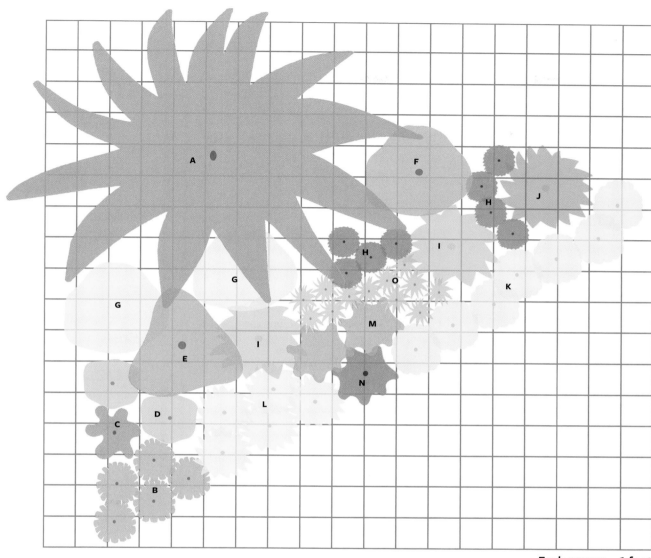

Each square = 1 foot

PLANT LIST

A. **1 Japanese maple** (*Acer palmatum*): Zones 5–8

B. **5 Siebold primrose** (*Primula sieboldii*): Zones 3–8

C. **1 Husker Red penstemon** (*Penstemon digitalis* 'Husker Red'): Zones 2–8

D. **2 Balloon flower** (*Platycodon grandiflorus*): Zones 4–9

E. **1 Pink rhododendron** (*Rhododendron* spp.): Zones 4–10

F. **1 Pink azalea** (*Rhododendron* spp.): Zones 4–10

G. **2 White azalea** (*Rhododendron* spp.): Zones 4–10

H. **8 Giant allium** (*Allium giganteum*): Zones 5–10

I. **2 June hosta** (*Hosta* 'June'): Zones 3–9

J. **1 Francee hosta** (*Hosta* 'Francee'): Zones 3–9

K. **7 Forget-me-not** (*Myosotis sylvatica*): Zones 5–9

L. **5 Astilbe** (*Astilbe* spp.): Zones 4–9

M. **2 Coralbell** (*Heuchera sanguinea*): Zones 4–8

N. **1 Purple Heuchera** (*Heuchera* spp.): Zones 4–8

O. **12 English bluebell** (*Hyacinthoides non-scripta*): Zones 4–9

Easy-Care Rose Garden

If you love roses, add them to your landscape. When you select low-maintenance rose species, you also minimize care.

Easy-care roses ring a white-columned porch.

It's a myth that roses are hard to grow; only certain types require coddling. Choose the right rose for your climate and it will be nearly maintenance-free. This garden plan features tough, fuss-free shrub roses—sturdy pink 'New Dawn', cardinal red Knock Out, and cerise pink 'William Baffin'. Team the shrub roses—selected for dependable vigor and long-lasting flowers—with an edging of stalwart perennial lady's mantle.

To grow shrub roses successfully, plant them in full sun, mulch the soil around them, and enjoy some of the most floriferous plants in your garden.

Planting roses

The time of year to plant roses depends on the region and the type of rose. Generally, plant container-grown roses any time of year except during temperature extremes. Avoid periods when hard freezes (below 25°F) or extended heat (over 90°F) are likely. In most regions, this means planting container-grown roses from early spring through autumn. In warm climates, plant them from fall through late winter.

In Zone 6 and colder, avoid planting container-grown roses in fall, which isn't enough time to establish before winter cold.

Bare-root roses have a narrower window for planting. They need temperate, moist conditions to get established. Plant bare-root roses in spring about the same time that other plants are leafing out, but before daytime temperatures regularly climb into the 80s. In the southern quarter of the United States, plant them in fall and winter.

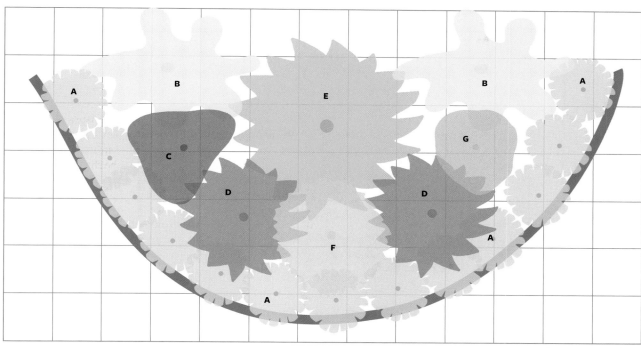

Each square = 1 foot

PLANT LIST

A. 13 Lady's mantle (*Alchemilla mollis*): Zones 4–8

B. 2 Light pink climbing rose (*Rosa* 'New Dawn'): Zones 5–9

C. 1 Red shrub rose (*Rosa* 'La Sevillana'): Zones 4–10

D. 2 Red shrub rose (*Rosa* Knock Out 'Radrazz'): Zones 4–10

E. 1 Deep pink shrub rose (*Rosa* 'William Baffin')*: Zones 3–8

F. 1 Light pink shrub rose (*Rosa* 'The Fairy'): Zones 4–9

G. 1 Apricot-pink shrub rose (*Rosa* 'Perdita'): Zones 4–9

* Climbing type also available.

Dress Up a Fence Garden

This low-care, sun-loving cottage garden is a rewarding introduction to perennial gardening. Enjoy color from spring to autumn.

Sunny yellow and orange nasturtiums scamper over the ground and through the fence. Purple and lavender delphiniums, blue-purple mallow, pink foxgloves, and pale yellow roses sprout from the colorful carpet. The display is so dense and flowers so plentiful that the white fence along the center of the garden nearly disappears. And because the plants are so densely mixed, there is little chance of weeds cropping up.

This arresting mix of annuals, long-blooming perennials, and roses incorporates a color theme. Four colors—purple, pink, yellow, and orange—predominate. Selecting flowers that bloom in different shades of the four colors keeps the scene engaging; mixing tall plants among short ones adds depth and generates interest on every level.

Capturing cottage style

Cottage gardens share a handful of characteristics.

Avoid too formal Most are a higgledy-piggledy mix of plants, the more eclectic the better. There are few rules for mixing and matching.

Think nonfussy Use plants that grow easily in your area. If they're divisions from friends and neighbors, so much the better.

Plant close and full Place plants close together so they tumble over one another. Position them slightly erratically.

Choose curvy and asymmetrical The less planned a garden looks, the more successfully it fits cottage style.

This gregarious mix of annuals and perennials transforms a fenceline into a cottage garden.

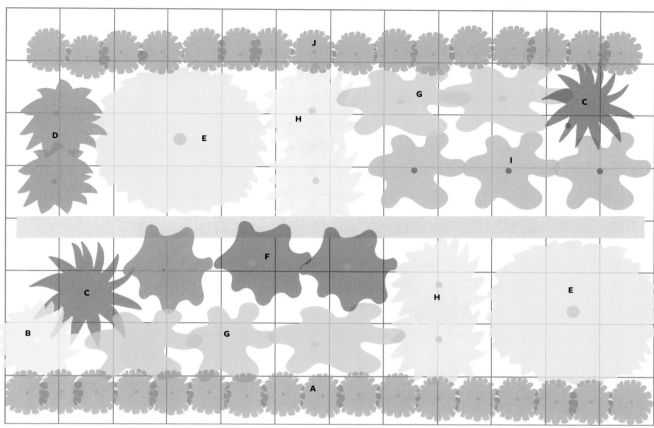

Each square = 1 foot

PLANT LIST

A. 17 Lobelia erinus: Annual

B. 1 Shasta daisy (*Leucanthemum × superbum*): Zones 4–9

C. 2 Bearded iris (*Iris × germanica*): Zones 3–10

D. 2 Brazilian verbena (*Verbena bonariensis*): Zones 7–11; annual elsewhere

E. 2 Rose (*Rosa* 'Peace'): Zones 5–9

F. 3 Delphinium 'Pacific Giant': Zones 3–7

G. 5 Nasturtium (*Tropaeolum* Gleam Series): Annual

H. 4 Spanish lavender (*Lavandula stoechas* subsp. *pedunculata*): Zones 8–11*

I. 3 Foxglove (*Digitalis purpurea*): Biennial Zones 4–9

J. 16 Impatiens walleriana: Annual

*In colder regions substitute English lavender.

Tough As Nails Perennial Garden

Lack of moisture and baking sun aren't problems when you select plants that can withstand weather-related abuse and still look lovely.

A focal point, such as a birdbath, creates a sense of unity in a small garden.

The beauty of planting perennials is that they come back each year and need little care except for an annual cleanup. This easy-care garden is filled with tough-as-nails perennials that get bigger and better each year.

If your garden doesn't receive much rain, don't worry. Instead of installing irrigation, choose plants that are naturally drought-tolerant. In this garden plan, the silvery green foliage of lavender and Russian sage creates a color-coordinated look. The foliage hues meld well with the blue birdbath, an eye-catching focal point as well as a way to add a touch of cooling moisture to the dry garden.

Most dry-climate plants demand excellent drainage, so where soils are heavy, work in plenty of compost or grit, such as sand, to help carry water away. Gravel is the mulch of choice for plants that need good drainage because it quickly drains excess water away from plant crowns—where stems meet the roots—to thwart fungal rot problems.

The beauty of a focal point

Any good garden design has a focal point or series of focal points, and it's an easy principle to put in place in landscape design for beginners. A focal point may be a birdbath, a piece of sculpture or art, a planted pot, or a stunning specimen plant or small tree. A focal point draws the eye into the garden.

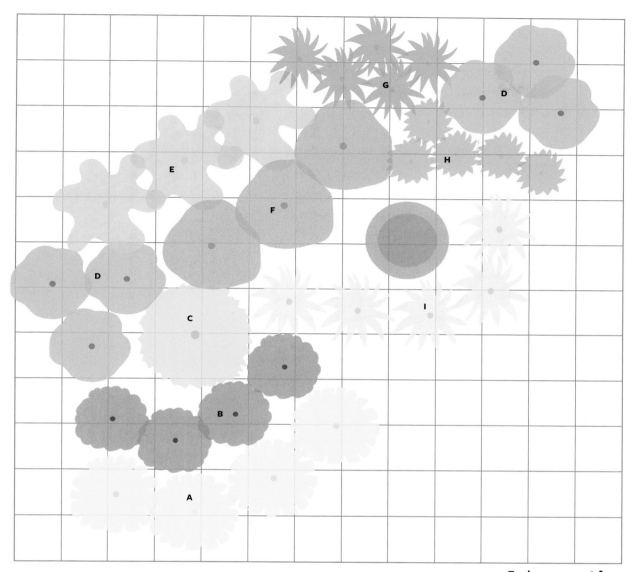

Each square = 1 foot

PLANT LIST

A. 4 Lavender cotton (*Santolina chamaecyparissus*): Zones 5–10

B. 4 English lavender (*Lavandula angustifolia* 'Munstead'): Zones 5–8

C. 1 Yarrow (*Achillea* 'Moonshine'): Zones 3–9

D. 6 Garden phlox (*Phlox paniculata*): Zones 4–8

E. 3 Russian sage (*Perovskia atriplicifolia*): Zones 5–9

F. 3 Purple coneflower (*Echinacea purpurea*): Zones 3–9

G. 5 Firecracker penstemon (*Penstemon eatonii*): Zones 4–9

H. 5 Pineleaf penstemon (*Penstemon pinifolius*): Zones 4–10

I. 5 Catmint (*Nepeta* × *faassenii*): Zones 3–8

Super-Easy Shade Garden

Lack of sun isn't a deterrent for a beautiful garden. Shaded areas can be lush and colorful with the right selection of plants.

The area along a grouping of trees provides the perfect setting for a shade garden. Soil is rich and shade is dappled. Shafts of sunlight support plants, such as black mondograss and daylilies, that can thrive in partial sun.

In this garden plan, variegated foliage of a red-twig dogwood brightens the scene with striking white-and-green leaves in summer and red twigs in winter and early spring. Trimming the shrub back to the ground in early spring keeps it on the short side and yields the reddest stems later in the season.

Hostas reign supreme in shady environs, where their leaf hues and variegations offer endless combinations. Showcase miniature types in partially buried pots so Lilliputian leaves aren't engulfed by surrounding plantings. Astilbe, with its striking foliage and flowers, earns a must-have mark for shade gardens.

This garden thrives in soil that's moist, rich, and well-drained. Create the right footing for plants by annually amending soil with compost and layering shredded leaves onto the garden in fall.

Planting near woodlands

Step up with shrubs Shrubs and small landscape trees help the eye adjust to taller woodland trees. A border of shrubs goes a long way to blend cultivated areas with woodland.

Go natural Accent the garden with nature-theme accessories. The stone in this garden is a good example. Also consider birdhouses, bee skeps, decorative bird feeders, driftwood, and small statues of woodland animals.

Outsmart the animals Rather than battle deer and rabbits, plant flowers and shrubs they avoid.

Variegated leaves, light-tone stones, and a medley of hostas in varying shades of green make shade shine. Perennials add blossoms to the setting throughout the growing season.

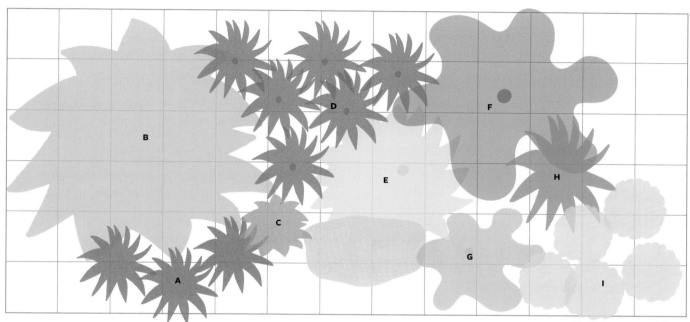

Each square = 1 foot

PLANT LIST

A. **3 Black mondograss**
(*Ophiopogon planiscapus*
'Nigrescens'): Zones 6–10

B. **1 Variegated redtwig
dogwood** (*Cornus alba*
'Elegantissima'): Zones 3–8

C. **1 Lily** (*Lilium* hybrids):
Zones 3–9

D. **6** *Astilbe × arendsii* **'Fanal'**:
Zones 4–8

E. **1 Hosta 'Frances Williams'**:
Zones 3–8

F. **1 Siebold hosta** (*Hosta
sieboldiana* var. *elegans*):
Zones 3–10

G. **1 Hosta 'Halcyon'**:
Zones 3–10

H. **1 Ostrich fern** (*Matteuccia
pennsylvanica*): Zones 2–9

I. **5 Impatiens walleriana:**
Annual

Low-Water Garden

Count on this minimal-fuss garden to look inviting even through dry spells.

A few weeks of watering right after planting is the only supplemental water this drought-tolerant garden requires. Once its roots are established, it will maintain its good looks through extended dry spells. Stocked with low-maintenance plants that thrive in full sun and dry, well-drained soil, the garden shines from spring to fall, thanks to a bevy of textures and long-blooming flowers.

Consider many places to plant this low-water wonder. A sunny spot near your home's foundation, along a driveway, and the streetside strip of grass in front of your home are all viable choices. Be sure to choose a site that receives at least eight hours of direct sun a day and has quick-draining soil.

Ornamental grasses and shrubs form the bones of the garden and frilly perennials fill in the gaps. Because most grasses are drought-tolerant, use your favorites. Choose feather reedgrass for an upright, stately look or maidengrass, with arching, silvery plumes, for a romantic appearance.

Drought-tolerant by design

With some clever design tricks, you can reduce the amount of water poured onto your landscape.

Group plants by water needs Create an oasis zone close to the house (and water source) for thirsty plants. Group plants that need only occasional watering farther out. Place the most self-sufficient plants at the perimeter of the property.

Reduce lawn Replace thirsty lawn grasses with beds and borders of ornamental grasses, low-water groundcovers, and drought-tolerant perennials and shrubs.

Create shade Plant trees that will have a high canopy and cast dappled shade. Or construct a lattice house, pergola, or other structure to cast shade.

Made up primarily of perennials, this drought-tolerant garden stays striking during long, hot days of summer.

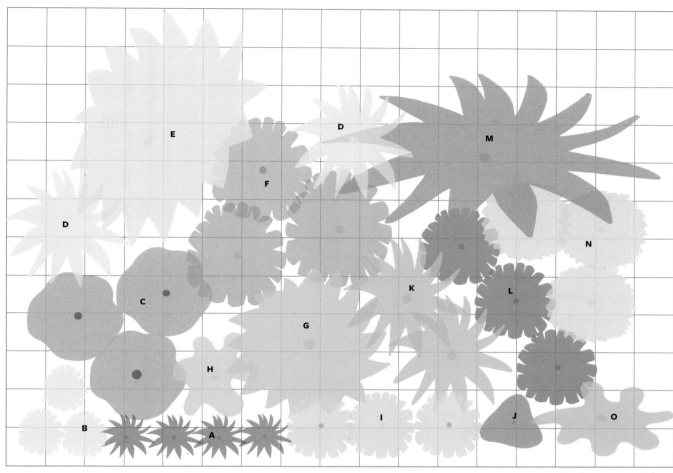

Each square = 1 foot

PLANT LIST

A. 4 Crested iris (*Iris cristata*): Zones 4–10

B. 3 Sweet alyssum (*Lobularia maritima*): Annual

C. 3 Sedum 'Autumn Joy': Zones 3–10

D. 2 Feather reedgrass (*Calamagrostis × acutiflora* 'Karl Foerster'): Zones 5–9

E. 1 Variegated redtwig dogwood (*Cornus alba* 'Elegantissima'): Zones 2–9

F. 3 New England aster (*Aster novae-angliae* 'Alma Pötschke'): Zones 4–8

G. 1 Spurge (*Euphorbia characias*): Zones 7–11

H. 1 Money plant (*Lunaria annua*): Zones 5–9; biennial*

I. 3 Lady's mantle (*Alchemilla mollis*): Zones 4–7

J. 1 Spotted deadnettle (*Lamium maculatum* 'White Nancy'): Zones 3–8

K. 2 Shrubby dusty miller (*Brachyglottis compacta*): Zones 8–11

L. 3 Stonecrop (*Sedum cauticola* 'Ruby Glow'): Zones 5–9

M. 1 Japanese barberry (*Berberis thunbergii* 'Rose Glow'): Zones 4–8

N. 3 Michaelmas daisy (*Aster novae-belgii* 'Lassie'): Zones 4–8

O. 1 Silver Carpet Lamb's-ears (*Stachys byzantina* 'Silver Carpet'): Zones 4–8

*A biennial grows only foliage the first year, flowers the second year, then dies after developing seeds.

USDA Plant Hardiness Zone Map

Each plant has an ability to withstand low temperatures. This range of temperatures is expressed as a Zone—and a Zone map shows where you can grow a plant.

Planting for your Zone

The U.S. Department of Agriculture designates 11 Zones from Canada to Mexico, and each represents the lowest expected winter temperature in that area. Each Zone is based on a 10°F difference in minimum temperatures. Once you know your hardiness Zone, you can choose plants for your garden that will flourish. Look for the hardiness Zone on the plant tags of the perennials, trees, and shrubs you buy.

Microclimates in your yard

Not all areas in your yard are the same. Depending on geography, trees, and structures, some spots may receive different sunlight and wind and consequently experience temperature differences. Take a look around your yard; you may notice that the same plant comes up sooner in one place than another. This is the microclimate concept in action. A microclimate is an area in your yard that is slightly different (cooler or warmer) than the other areas of your yard.

Create a microclimate

Once you're aware of your yard's microclimates, use them to your advantage. For example, you may be able to grow plants in a sheltered, south-facing garden bed that you can't grow elsewhere in your yard. You can create a microclimate by planting evergreens on the north side of a property to block prevailing winds. Or plant deciduous trees on the south side to provide shade in summer.

Range of Average Annual Minimum Temperatures for Each Zone

Source: U.S. Department of Agriculture

- Zone 1: below -50°F (below -45°C)
- Zone 2: -50 to -40°F (-45 to -40°C)
- Zone 3: -40 to -30°F (-40 to -35°C)
- Zone 4: -30 to -20°F (-35 to -29°C)

- Zone 5: -20 to -10°F (-29 to -23°C)
- Zone 6: -10 to 0°F (-23 to -18°C)
- Zone 7: 0 to 10°F (-18 to -12°C)
- Zone 8: 10 to 20°F (-12 to -7°C)

- Zone 9: 20 to 30°F (-7 to -1°C)
- Zone 10: 30 to 40°F (-1 to 4°C)
- Zone 11: 40°F and above (4°C and above)

Index

Page references in italics denote photographs.